KINDLY
INQUISITORS

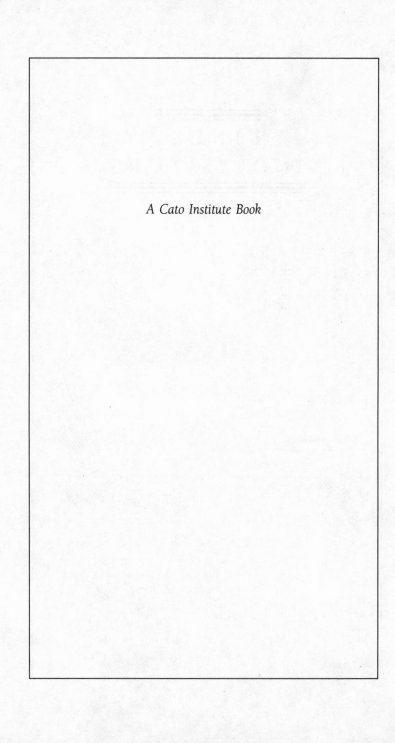

A Cato Institute Book

KINDLY INQUISITORS

The New Attacks on Free Thought

JONATHAN RAUCH

The University of Chicago Press

Chicago and London

The University of Chicago Press, Chicago 60637
The University of Chicago Press, Ltd., London
© 1993 by Jonathan Rauch
All rights reserved. Published 1993
Printed in the United States of America
02 01 00 99 98 97 96 95 94 93   2 3 4 5
ISBN: 0-226-70575-7 (cloth)

Library of Congress Cataloging-in-Publication Data

Rauch, Jonathan, 1960-
    Kindly inquisitors : the new attacks on free thought / Jonathan
        Rauch. p.   cm.
    "A Cato Institute book."
    Includes index.
        1. Censorship—United States.   2. United States—Intellectual
    life—20th century.   I. Title.
    Z658.U5P38   1993
    323.44'0973—dc20   92-35805
                                                            CIP

This book is printed on acid-free paper.

═══════════════

IN MEMORIAM

Salman Rushdie

June 1947–February 1989

Et expecto

resurrectionem

mortuorum

Upon this first, and in one sense this
sole, rule of reason, that in order to
learn you must desire to learn, and
in so desiring not be
satisfied with what you already
incline to think, there follows one
corollary, which itself deserves to be
inscribed upon every wall
of the city of philosophy:

Do not block the way of inquiry.

—*Charles Sanders Peirce*

CONTENTS

ACKNOWLEDGMENTS

Among the many people who have helped with this book, a few require special thanks: Christopher C. DeMuth of the American Enterprise Institute and David Boaz of the Cato Institute, whose support made the book possible; the Esther A. and Joseph Klingenstein Fund, which helped finance my research; David Hull, for intellectual generosity far beyond the call of duty; and Donald Richie, who kept the faith.

1

New Threats to Free Thought

In 1990 the French national assembly passed new laws to toughen the existing measures against racism. At the time people were in an uproar over the desecration of Jewish graves in France, and the newspapers were full of concern about France's extremist right wing and the revival of anti-Semitism in Europe and the Soviet Union. So the new legislation surprised no one. But there was something disturbing in it, passed over incidentally, as though hardly worth mentioning, in newspaper accounts like this one: "The measures also outlaw 'revisionism'—a historical tendency rife among extreme right-wing activists which consists of questioning the truth of the Jewish Holocaust in World War II."

Some of those words stir memories: "measures" that "outlaw . . . questioning." We have seen that before.

Taken by itself, the French action was a curious and vaguely troubling incident, but little more. The intentions were good, and it is a fact that many and probably most of the so-called Holocaust "revisionists" were Jew-haters and Jew-baiters who were acting in bad faith, and it is a fact also that the Holocaust *did* happen; so let the matter pass. Fair enough.

No. The French action could not be taken by itself. It was part of a pattern.

In Australia the New South Wales parliament amended the Anti-Discrimination Act in 1989 to ban public racial vilification. Since most people are against racial vilification, most could sympathize with the legislature's intentions. But it was hard to be enthusiastic about the mechanism: "The law invests in the Anti-Discrimination Board the power to determine whether a report is 'fair,' and whether a discussion is 'reasonable,' 'in good faith,' and 'in the public interest.' The Board will pronounce upon the acceptability of artistic expression, research papers, academic controversy, and scientific questions. An unfair (i.e., inaccurate) report of a public act may expose the reporter and the publisher to damages of up to $40,000."[1]

In Austria you can get a prison sentence for denying the existence of the Nazi gas chambers. In 1992 the government, seeking to make the offense clearer, proposed language which would make it a crime "to deny, grossly minimize, praise or justify through printed works, over the airwaves or in any other medium the National Socialist genocide or any other National Socialist crime."[2] In Denmark the national civil-rights law forbids "threatening, humiliating, or degrading" someone in public on the basis of race, religion, ethnic background, or sexual orientation. When a woman wrote letters to a newspaper calling the national domestic-partnership law "ungodly" and homosexuality "the ugliest kind of adultery," she and the editor who published her letters were targeted for prosecution.[3] In Great Britain the Race Relations Act forbids speech that expresses racial hatred, "not only when it is likely to lead to violence, but generally, on the grounds that members of minority races should be protected from racial insults."[4]

In Canada a reputable research psychologist named Jean Philippe Rushton presented a paper in 1989 in which he looked at three very broad racial groups and hypothesized that, on average, blacks' reproductive strategy tends to emphasize high birthrates, Asians' tends toward intensive parental nurturing, and whites' tends to fall in between. The man was vilified in the press, he was denounced on national television (to his face) as a neo-Nazi, and his graduate students were advised to find a new mentor. That was not all. The Ontario provincial police promptly launched a six-month investigation of Rushton under Canada's hate-speech prohibition. They questioned his colleagues, demanded tapes of his debates and media appearances, and so on. "The provincial police officially assessed the question of whether Rushton might be subject to two years in prison for such actions as 'using questionable source data.' "[5]

So it goes in France, Australia, Austria, Canada—and the United States. In the United States, however, there is an important difference. The U.S. Constitution makes government regulation of upsetting talk difficult. There is not much the government can do to silence offensive speech or obnoxious criticism. In America, therefore, the movement against hurtful speech has been primarily moral rather than legal, and nongovernmental institutions, especially colleges and universities, have taken the lead. All around the country, universities have set up anti-harassment rules prohibiting, and establishing punishments for, "speech or other expression" (this is from Stanford's policy, adopted in 1990 and more or less representative) which "is intended to insult or stigmatize an individual or a small number of individuals on the basis of their sex, race, color, handicap, religion, sexual orientation or national and ethnic origin."[6]

Those rules are being enforced. One case became particularly well known, because it generated a lawsuit in the federal courts, which eventually struck down the rule in question. At the University of Michigan, a student said in a classroom discussion that he considered homosexuality a disease treatable with therapy. Now, as of this writing the evidence is abundant that the student's hypothesis is wrong, and any gay man or woman in America can attest to the harm that this particular hypothesis has inflicted over the years. But the people at Michigan went further than to refute the student or ignore him. They summoned him to a formal disciplinary hearing for violating the school's policy prohibiting speech that "victimizes" people on the basis of "sexual orientation."[7]

What is disturbing is not just that this sort of thing happened, but that it happens all the time now and intellectual opinion often supports it. The Michigan incident was just one among many. In 1990 at Southern Methodist University, "five white students and one black student reported to university officials that a freshman had denounced Dr. [Martin Luther] King as a Communist and had sung 'We Shall Overcome' in a sarcastic manner during a late-night discussion in a residence hall."[8] A university judicial board sentenced the offending freshman to thirty hours of community service at minority organizations.

Cases of that kind are controversial—off campus, at least—and are drawing their share of outrage from civil libertarians. However, to understand the French and Australian and Michigan incidents as raising only civil-liberties issues is to miss the bigger point. A very dangerous principle is now being established as a social right: Thou shalt not hurt others with words. This principle is a menace—and not just to civil liberties. At bottom it threatens liberal inquiry—that is, science itself.

If that statement sounds too alarmist, I won't contest the point here but will ask you to read on. I will ask you, also, to remember this: In English we have a word for the empanelment of tribunals—public or private, but in any case prestigious and powerful—to identify and penalize false and socially dangerous opinions. The word applies reasonably well to a system in which a university student is informed against, and then summoned to a hearing and punished, for making incorrect and hurtful remarks during a conversation late at night. The word has been out of general circulation for many years. It is "inquisition."

This book is about the liberal social system for sorting truth from falsehood: arguably our greatest and most successful political system. It is also about that system's political enemies: not only the ancient enemies, the old-fashioned authoritarians, but also the newer ones, the egalitarians and humanitarians. It is partly a book about free speech, to the extent that the principles it discusses affect laws and governments' policies. But enough has been written elsewhere in defense of the First Amendment. This book tries to defend the morality, rather than the legality, of a knowledge-producing social system which often causes real suffering to real people. It tries to defend the liberal intellectual system against a rising anti-critical ideology.

We have standard labels for the liberal political and economic systems—democracy and capitalism. Oddly, however, we have no name for the liberal intellectual system, whose activities range from physics to history to journalism. So in this book I use the term "liberal science," for reasons to be explained later. The very need to invent a label for our public idea-sorting system speaks volumes about the system's success. Establishing the principles on which liberal science is based required a social revolution; yet so effective have those principles been, and so beneficent, that most of us take them for granted. We rarely take the time to stop and cherish them, any more than we stop to cherish the right to own property or to vote—less so, indeed. The liberal regime for making knowledge is not something most of us have ever even thought about. That fact is a tribute to its success. Sadly, it is also a reason so many Americans are dozing through the current attack.

And just what kind of "attack" is going on? Let me try to make it clearer in the following way.

The question which forms the central issue of this book is, What should be society's principle for raising and settling differences of opinion? In other words, what is the right way, or at least the best way, to make decisions as to who is right (thus having knowledge) and who is wrong (thus having mere opinion)?

There are a million ways to ask that question, and they come up every day. On May 10, 1989, the Nashville *Tennessean* reported that George Darden, a city councilman, had filed a resolution asking the city to build a landing pad for unidentified flying objects. "What it was," he said, "people were reporting all these strange creatures coming to town, and they have nowhere to land." He said that he had never seen the creatures himself but that he was "very serious." He wanted to know, "When people see them, do you want to just cast them off as a lunatic?"

George Darden was no clown. He was raising nothing less than what philosophers refer to as the problem of knowledge: What is the right standard for distinguishing the few true beliefs from the many false ones? And who should set that standard? Everybody laughed at George Darden—but he deserves an answer. After all, what is a politician supposed to do when his constituents start reporting UFOs?

To the central question of how to sort true beliefs from the "lunatic" ones, here are five answers, five decision-making principles—not the only principles by any means, but the most important contenders right now:

● *The Fundamentalist Principle:* Those who know the truth should decide who is right.

● *The Simple Egalitarian Principle:* All sincere persons' beliefs have equal claims to respect.

● *The Radical Egalitarian Principle:* Like the simple egalitarian principle, but the beliefs of persons in historically oppressed classes or groups get special consideration.

● *The Humanitarian Principle:* Any of the above, but with the condition that the first priority be to cause no hurt.

● *The Liberal Principle:* Checking of each by each through public criticism is the only legitimate way to decide who is right.

The argument of this book is that the last principle is the *only* one which is acceptable, but that it is now losing ground to the others, and that this development is extremely dangerous. Impelled by the notions that science is oppression and criticism is violence, the central regulation of debate and inquiry is returning to respectability—this time in a humanitarian disguise. In America, in France, in Austria and Australia and elsewhere, the old principle of the Inquisition is being revived: people who hold wrong and hurtful opinions should be punished for the good of society. If they cannot be put in jail, then they should lose their jobs, be subjected to organized campaigns of vilification, be made to apologize, be pressed to recant. If government cannot do the punishing, then private institutions and pressure groups—thought vigilantes, in effect—should do it.

Strange, fully three and a half centuries after the Roman Catholic Inquisition arrested and tried Galileo, to be writing about a new anti-critical ideology, and about public and private movements to enforce it. Strange to use words like "Inquisition" and "thought vigilantes." What has happened? And why now?

Consider, then, the stories of two new challenges to liberal science. One story is about fairness, the other about compassion.

The story about fairness begins in the last century, when the strong claims of conservative religious forces finally collapsed under the onslaught of Lyell and Darwin and T. H. Huxley and the whole implacable advance of establishment science. God and the Bible had long since been mostly banished from physics and astronomy. The last redoubts were geology and biology, the histories of the earth and of life; the Bible, after all, said little about the laws of motion but a great deal about the creation of the world and its occupants. Yet even in the life sciences and earth sciences, time was running out for those who believed in religious authority. By the 1830s even pious geologists like the Reverend Adam Sedgwick were declaring that there was no evidence of a worldwide Noachian flood. The Bible, he and others said, simply could not be taken literally. If one read between the lines, they were saying that the Bible was only for moral guidance, not for knowledge of the world around us.

Twenty years after the publication of Darwin's *Origin of Species* in 1859, there was hardly a naturalist in the world who did not support some version of evolutionary theory.[9] Yet the public was much slower to come around to evolution than the scholars. The new scientific consensus left millions of ordinary people behind. To fundamentalist Christians in particular, the issue was a moral one. In the 1920s they led a crusade to evict ungodly evolutionism from the public schools, and by the end of the decade four states had banned the teaching of Darwinism and more than twenty had considered doing so. Among the states that had adopted the ban was Tennessee, where the law was challenged in the famous Scopes trial of 1925. The ban was upheld, but the fundamentalists' leader, William Jennings Bryan, was humiliated on the witness stand, the press mocked the anti-evolutionists, and by the end of the decade anti-evolutionism had run out of steam. The movement turned inward and sank almost—though not quite—into oblivion.

When liberal Americans like me and, probably, you look at the creationists of that day, we see a gang of ignorant troglodytes out to abolish progress. But surely we commit an injustice if we fail to think how terrible it must be to see one's holy book dragged through the mud and an ungodly secular idol erected in its place. The creationists were trying to defend their world, their decency.

They failed, utterly. But their complaint did not go away; it gnawed like a stomachache. The creationists, indeed, began to see that they had done worse than to lose the battle for supremacy; they had lost even the battle to have their beliefs considered an equally legitimate alternative. In the 1960s came a revival of creationism, but this time with a twist. It was "creation *science*" now, they said: an alternative theory. As had been the case in the decades before, scientists and liberal intellectuals dismissed creation science with a laugh; hardly any reputable scholars would go anywhere near it. It was the old biblical story purged of all references to God or the Bible and dressed up with such scraps of evidence, real or imagined, as could be gathered. But the public was more receptive than the professionals. And in the 1970s the creationists discovered an appealing new cause: Equal time for creationism!

They argued that evolution was religion just as much as creation, and they argued that "creation science" was just as scientific as "evolution science." They even argued that creationism was more scientific than evolution. They argued every which way, but the point was always the same: there is more than one way to view the world, and all we want (they said) is a little fairness, a chance to make our case.

Although it was often dismissed casually, their position in fact had deep philosophical strength. Science and skeptical inquiry are one path to belief about the world; looking in the Bible or consulting your guru is another. If both paths are subject to uncertainty—as skeptical science must admit!—then why not present them both in the classroom, as alternatives? Why grant privileges? "Your belief in, say, Darwin's theory rests, finally, no less on faith—faith in science—than does my belief in special creation; and so on what grounds can you claim a monopoly on truth, since my beliefs are held just as strongly and as sincerely as yours?"

Thus the creationists began to portray themselves as an oppressed minority. "Under the present system . . . the student is being indoctrinated in a philosophy of secular humanism," one typical creationist complained. "The authoritarianism of the medieval church has been replaced by the authoritarianism of rational materialism. Constitutional guarantees are violated and free scientific inquiry is stifled under this blanket of dogmatism."[10] That is what a fundamentalist Christian state education official in Arizona was getting at when he said that if parents tell their children that the earth is flat, teachers have no right to contradict them. No one has a right to impose his opinion on others—and the idea that humans evolved from earlier species is, the Christians said, ultimately just some people's opinion. A common opinion, true; the experts' opinion, true. But minorities have rights, and experts can be wrong.

In response to their complaint, they got little but scorn from the establishment. When a creationist protests that what is being tossed in the ditch happens to be the truth about human genesis, he is told, "Well, you're wrong." Then when he asks what gives *you* the right to set the standard for truth, he is told, "Because we're right." And when he begs to know why his view of the world should not at least be presented as a fair alternative, someone will tell him, "Because you're a nut." Those are bad answers, arrogant and self-dealing. It is quite useless to pretend that it is "fair," in the sense of evenhanded, to kick someone's beliefs out of the canon if they do not happen to be deemed science by the intellectual establishment. If we on the Darwinian side of the question are going to insist on preferential treatment for our way of looking at the world (and we should), and if in the process we are going to cause pain and outrage to people who do not happen to look at the world our way, then we had better have an awfully good reason—a much better reason than "Because we're right and you're wrong and that's that." If we do not, then shame on us.

But dismissed the creationists' complaint was. They lost a court case in 1982 when Arkansas's Balanced Treatment for Creation-Science and Evolution-Science Act was struck down by a federal judge as unconstitutionally injecting religious instruction into public schools. They lost again over a similar law in Louisiana—this time before the U.S. Supreme Court.[11] Yet the Supreme Court decision brought a dissent from two justices who argued passionately that a majority was indeed oppressing a minority. And elsewhere there were signs of softening in the face of the creationists' demands for fairness. In November 1989 the California state board of education, under pressure from evangelical Christians, adopted textbook guidelines that deleted a reference to evolution as "scientific fact." (The nature of the process by which evolution works remains a matter of some controversy, but the occurrence of evolution, the *fact* of evolution, is as settled as any proposition in science.) Banished from the guidelines was the true statement "There is no scientific dispute that evolution has occurred and continues to occur; this is why evolution is regarded as scientific fact" and also "These sequences show that life has continually diversified through time, as older species have been replaced by newer ones."[12]

There was a reason for the softening. Fair-minded observers had to admit that the creationists were on to something. It was one thing to demand supremacy, but quite another to demand equal time. Why should the evolutionary, "officially" scientific story be the *only* legitimate story? No less a personage than Ronald Reagan himself said that if evolution was going to be taught, then the biblical story of creation should also be taught; one poll found that three-fourths of the public agreed with him.

If the story ended there it would not be so very interesting. But in the 1970s and especially the 1980s it acquired a new dimension. The battle for intellectual "fairness"—for the Egalitarian Principle— was joined by a new and more powerful faction.

By the 1980s the creationists were not alone. Exactly the same line of attack was now being pursued by their enemies on the political left. What about minority viewpoints? Why were they not being taught, at least as valid alternatives to the all-male, all-European tradition of "mainstream" history and social science? "Native people say they were created here, that they sprang from Earth, not from Europe or Asia," said one activist. "Why not give those theories equal time? To present theory as truth and disregard people's religious beliefs is racist."[13] In 1989 a task force on minorities reported to the New York state education commissioner that "African-Americans, Asian-Americans, Puerto Ricans/Latinos, and native Americans have all been the victims of an intellectual and educational oppression that has characterized the culture and institutions of the United States and the European-American world for centuries."[14] The task force said that even when dealing with topics like the writing of the Constitution, curriculum developers must find a contribution from every major ethnic group.[15] The creationists had argued that the question of human creation was too important to be monopolized by professional biologists, who are biased by dint of being secular humanists. Now came others arguing that the question of America's constitutional heritage was too important to be left to the conventional historians, who are biased by dint of being privileged white males.

Here again were charges of indoctrination, of alternative points of view being oppressed and locked out. Because of their Eurocentric worldview, "the education systems in New York State and throughout the United States of America have produced processes of 'miseducation' that must be challenged and changed."[16] A growing number of minority activists were rejecting outright the legitimacy of the mainstream scientific and intellectual establishment ("white European" science). One television producer said, "African-Americans are now smart enough to know that historically we have been written out of history, and so we are not waiting for the approval of white scholars to believe the research that these African and African-American scholars have done."[17] There was evolution science, creation science, male science, female science, white science, black science. It was about this time when people took to wearing T-shirts with the slogan "It's a black thing. You wouldn't understand."

Thus the rise of minority activists' version of the creationist argument. They said that classical scholarship had lied about blacks' role in history—for example, about the African ethnicity of the ancient Egyptians. An outline for "multicultural" curriculum reform, adopted in various school districts, said that Africa—specifically Egypt—was "the world center of culture and learning in antiquity" and that ancient Egypt was a black nation. Leave aside why it should matter what color people were; the agenda here was to use political pressure to obtain at least equal time for an "outsiders'" viewpoint—the creationists' agenda precisely. As it was with creationism, the science of the matter was dubious. As to the claim that ancient Egypt was a black nation, the essayist John Leo reported that he "phoned seven Egyptologists at random around the country, and all seven said it is completely untrue, then asked that their names not be used. 'It's politically too hot to say this [in public],' said one."[18] (Not so long ago, there were parts of the United States where a biologist had to have some courage

to say outright that creationism was bunk.) Undoubtedly, there will
be more such claims as other interest groups demand respect and
attention for their own versions of the facts.

Adding strength to the challenge was that fair-minded academics
were also coming around. They produced an egalitarian argument
far more sophisticated than anything the creationists had been able
to develop. It goes more or less as follows:

Not to be biased is not to be human. We are all biased and
interested, we all have preferences, an intellectual temperament, and
a point of view; it is only that our biases go in different directions.
The secular Western notion of objectivity, of how to sort reality from
myth, has prevailed largely by a kind of imperialism—by trampling
on other traditions and stepping on the aspirations of women and
Africans and Asians and others who were excluded from European
male culture. The Zande who believes he is a witch or the Bororo
who asserts he is a red macaw or the Christian who believes the Bible
is literally true—none of those is a "lunatic" at all, but merely a
minority, a victim of the scientific order's hegemony, shut out by
dint of weakness. Science embodies a white European worldview,
and to impose it or insist on it, or to deny the equal merit of other
ways of thinking, is a form of domination. The biologist and feminist
theorist Ruth Hubbard says, in a phrase that could come from any
of a variety of contemporary writers on knowledge, "The pretense
that science is objective, apolitical and value-neutral is profoundly
political."[19] Which is to say, she adds, that the scientific method "rests
on a particular definition of objectivity that we feminists must call into
question"—a definition very much a culprit in the social exclusion of
women, nonwhites, and other minorities. (She might have added
fundamentalist Christians, but did not.)

In all honesty, one must confess that there is justice in this challenge. Any system for deciding who is objectively right is a social
system and so has political consequences. Liberal science does not
throw its opponents in jail, but it does deny their beliefs respectability,
and to deny respectability is to cause anguish and outrage. In the
modern West, the liberal, scientific view of knowledge *has* asserted
a unique claim to legitimacy, and that *is* a form of intellectual imperial-

ism, as is *any* person's or system's claim to special legitimacy in sorting true beliefs from false ones. Anyone who doubts that this is so might ponder the fate of Christian Scientists in today's America.

On December 4, 1984, a four-year-old girl named Natalie died very painfully of an infection. The cause was a common bacterium that is almost always killed by antibiotics. Her parents, however, did not use antibiotics; they used prayer. To many of us, that sounds preposterous. But imagine what it is to believe fervently in the healing power of your Lord. Imagine that your child is sick, and you want the best treatment, the one that is right and most likely to work. That treatment is prayer, or so you believe with all your heart. And that treatment you use. "We say those parents chose the method of care they felt was the most likely to make their child well," a church official said; and unquestionably he was right.

Then the child dies, and the parents are charged with manslaughter and child endangerment. Over the last ten years there have been dozens of such cases. In 1990 a two-year-old boy named Robyn died of a bowel obstruction after a five-day illness; his parents, David and Ginger Twitchell, were convicted of manslaughter and sentenced to ten years' probation. Pictures in the paper showed the mother, after the trial, cowering in her husband's arms as he faced news photographers. David Twitchell said, "If I try a method of care I think is working, I will stick with that. If I think it's not working, I will try something else."[20] By his own lights, he had done his best for his child. Anyone who did not happen to share the worldview of medical science could only view the prosecution and conviction of the Twitchells as the most blatant kind of scientific imperialism. True, in Robyn's case and Natalie's the prayer treatment had failed. But sometimes antibiotics and surgery fail, too. When surgery fails, should parents be put on trial for not having first tried prayer?

People like the Twitchells feel the full force of the liberal intellectual system's power to declare who is right and who is wrong. They know what it means to be declared losers in the game of science. Tell them about liberalism's being "tolerant" and they will snicker. The truth is that liberal science insists absolutely on freedom of belief and speech, but *freedom of knowledge it rejects absolutely*. When we are deciding whether or not a medical treatment is effective, we turn to liberal science and reject all other claimants. That is why Christian Scientists who unsuccessfully treat their children with prayer are charged with manslaughter, while parents who unsuccessfully try surgery are not. Is that "fair"?

If we do not have an answer to the demands for fairness, if we cannot justify the imperialism of liberal science and the refusal to recognize the validity of other systems, then we are forced to admit that the scientific order is indeed nothing more than the rule of the strong. In that case we must concede that David and Ginger Twitchell were in fact political prisoners, condemned because they and their fellow churchmen lacked the strength or numbers to impose on society *their* idea of truth. That is the egalitarian challenge.

Another challenge was also emerging. Though it advanced on a separate track, ultimately it would lead to much the same place as the challenge from fairness. This was the challenge from compassion.

America, like every country, has always had its share of bluenoses. H. L. Mencken taunted them as Puritans—people driven by the "haunting fear that someone, somewhere, may be happy." Their favorite target was pornography, which they attacked in the name of godliness and later decency and family values. Like the creationists, they came to be deplored and ridiculed by the intellectual establishment; but as did the creationists, they made an argument whose deep strength was unanswered and ignored for too long.

The claim of the bluenoses was that pornography was hurtful because it eroded morality and so was a menace to society. Opponents of bans on obscenity often pointed out that the line between smut and art, between the obscene and the beautiful, was impossible to draw, even in principle. And they pointed out that because there was no line, bans on the gross would also reach serious art—a point which was timelessly proved by the banning of Joyce's *Ulysses* in Great Britain and America, where shipments of the book were seized by the authorities and burned.

Yet battles like the one to save *Ulysses* from the bluenoses were soon won, with the help of liberal courts. Today, every so often the bluenoses resurface, as they always will. In 1989 came the high-visibility trial of the director of Cincinnati's Contemporary Art Center for showing homoerotic photographs by Robert Mapplethorpe, and in 1990 members of the rap group 2 Live Crew were tried for their explicit and rank lyrics.[21] But by the 1980s the anti-pornography activists no longer controlled the terms of debate; the presumption was against them, except perhaps where public money was involved.

Once again, however, the story was not over. Alongside and under-lying the puritanical moral fear was the objection that people and communities were being *hurt* by foul words or gross images. And that argument did not go away as society grew more permissive of pornography. Instead, the argument slept in a pupal cocoon and then reemerged stronger than before.

The context was again pornography. But this time the attack was more sophisticated and it came from feminists, not from bluenoses. The feminists' argument bears a moment of examination, because it soon became part of a broader pattern.

The core argument was that pornography hurt women by degrad-ing them, aiding in their repression, denying them their rights. Por-nography, said the influential feminist critic and scholar Catharine A. MacKinnon in 1983, "causes attitudes and behaviors of violence and discrimination that define the treatment and status of half of the population."[22] Real people were being hurt. Mary S. or Beth W. was raped or killed by a filth-inspired criminal. And against the actuality of those real-life horrors, the traditionalist male power structure was upholding the rights of pornographers to traffic in scenes of sexual violence and domination. The feminists were incredulous. Here, they said, was one more sign of the patriarchy's contempt for the human rights of women.

They made some inroads. Spurred by MacKinnon and others, the city of Indianapolis enacted an anti-pornography statute making pornography actionable as sex discrimination. (The law was later ruled unconstitutional.) By 1989 legislation to similar effect had been introduced in Congress. If you were the victim of a sex crime, and if you could show a link between the crime against you and some "specific pornographic material," then the legislation would give you the right to sue the material's maker or distributor for damages.[23] Setting aside the constitutional problems with such a law, the logic seemed compelling: if you are hurt, you can sue.

The trouble was that particular individuals were raped and bruised by criminals, not by dirty movies. "No respectable study or evidence has shown any causal link between pornography and actual violence."[24] "In countries where pornography is legalized, the crime rates for rape and sex offenses have actually decreased, according to a Danish report."[25] Showing a connection between any particular crime and any particular piece of pornography was difficult or impossible. Anyway, traditional doctrine said that you punish the criminal, not the ideas which might have been in his head or the person who might have put them there. Should selling *Mein Kampf* be illegal because some cretin read it and then killed a Jew? Traditional doctrine said, Certainly not. Nor should selling the Bible be illegal because someone reading the story of Cain and Abel might kill his brother, or someone reading "Thou shalt not suffer a witch to live" might kill a woman, or someone reading the story of Elisha (2 Kings 2:24) might kill rude children. To ban books or words which cretins find exciting is to let the very lowest among us determine what we may read or hear.

Faced with problems like those, feminists broadened their argument; and here is where, for our purposes, the argument gets especially interesting. The issue was not only that particular people might be hurt by particular crimes inspired by particular dirty books or movies. The issue was also that pornography hurt women *as a class*. "It does hurt individuals, not *as* individuals in a one-at-a-time sense, but as members of the group 'women,'" MacKinnon said.[26]

Pornography, in the feminist view, is a form of forced sex, a practice of sexual politics, an institution of gender inequality. In this perspective, pornography is not harmless fantasy or a corrupt and confused misrepresentation of an otherwise natural and healthy sexuality. Along with the rape and prostitution in which it participates, pornography institutionalizes the sexuality of male supremacy, which fuses the erotization of dominance and submission with the social construction of male and female. Gender is sexual. Pornography constitutes the meaning of that sexuality. Men treat women as who they see women being. Pornography constructs who that is.[27]

In other words, by portraying male domination of women, pornography transmits the ethic of male supremacy and makes it real. Thus pornography *in itself*—never mind any crimes which it might (or might not) inspire—oppresses women.

You may ask for evidence of such harm; but you should not expect to find it, because one of pornography's harms is to hide the damage it does. "If pornography is an act of male supremacy, its harm is the harm of male supremacy made difficult to see because of its pervasiveness, potency, and success in making the world a pornographic place. . . . To the extent pornography succeeds in constructing social reality, it becomes *invisible as harm.*"[28] In the world constructed by pornography, people who are not radical feminists can no more see the harm of pornography than a fish can see water. How, then, do we know if pornography is really doing the harm that feminists allege? Because it must be. By its very nature—by the images it expresses and the psychological climate it creates—pornography is oppressive.

I linger here because something interesting is going on. An old complaint against standard free-speech theory is that it lets people say harmful things (e.g., "You can get AIDS from a dirty toilet seat"). And the old reply is that "harmful" is in the eye of the beholder, and that while harmful actions should be punished, words and expressive images are the coin of opinion and thought and so are special. I can say "Republicans should be rounded up and shot," but I cannot have Republicans rounded up and shot. But now the complexion of the argument was changing. MacKinnon, in the passages quoted above and others, was within a metaphysician's eyelash of saying, not that pornography *causes* hurt, but that it *is* hurt. It *is* violence: specifically, it is *group* violence against women. And, sure enough, MacKinnon again and again wrote of pornography as an act. It is "an act of male supremacy," it is the sexist social order's "quintessential social act," it "is a political practice," it "is a form of forced sex," it "is more

actlike than thoughtlike," it is "a practice of sex discrimination," and
so on.[29]

The old, and admittedly sometimes tricky, distinction between
talk and action was being methodically blurred—and not just in
theory. In 1980, influenced by feminist legal theorists, the U.S. Equal
Employment Opportunity Commission adopted three tests for deciding whether speech in the workplace constitutes sexual harassment
punishable under civil-rights laws. Among those tests was whether
the words at issue create an "intimidating, hostile, or offensive working
environment." If words make the social situation uncomfortable for
somebody, the commission seemed to be saying, then they are not
mere words at all; rather, they are acts of harassment (just as pornography is an act of oppression).

So here was a theory which said that images and expressions and
words could be, for all practical purposes, a form of hurt or violence.
Keep your eye on this theory. Remember its face: you will see it
again.

In the 1980s it began to be commonplace for activists and intellectuals to conspicuously take offense. Here, there, everywhere, they
were offended. People began demanding public apologies when they
were offended. Often jokes were the target. Organized groups—gay
activists, for instance—began patrolling the presses and airwaves for
offensive statements and promptly demanding apologies and retrac-
tions when they found cause for complaint. "From gays to American
Indians to Asians to the disabled to environmentalists," reported the
Washington Post, "Hollywood at the end of 1991 seems besieged by
interest groups." In hopes of staying out of trouble, producers in
Hollywood began vetting their screenplays with activists before shoot-
ing, to make sure, as one producer said, that the film "has nothing
they would find offensive."[30] Activists began compiling and distribut-
ing lists of "offensive" expressions. (From the University of Missouri
journalism school's *Dictionary of Cautionary Words and Phrases:* "*Burly:*
An adjective too often associated with large black men, implying
ignorance, and considered offensive in this context. *Buxom:* Offensive
reference to a woman's chest. Do not use. See 'Woman.' *Codger:*
Offensive reference to a senior citizen.")[31] Professors began to tape

their classes in case they were charged with saying something offensive. As more and more people realized that they could win concessions and moral victories by being offended, more and more offended people became activists.

All of those activists were perfectly well within their legal rights, and no legal attempt was made to stop them. Nor did there seem to be any moral reason to want to stop them. Indeed, they seemed to have occupied the moral high ground. One could dismiss them as the new Puritans, the new bluenoses, which in part they were. But they were also acting on morally unimpeachable motives: to protect the weak, to salve hurt feelings, and to weed out hateful and hurtful ideas—racist ideas, sexist ideas, homophobic or unpatriotic ideas. There was to be no place in civil society for people who said "nigger" or "queer" (or "burly" or "buxom"), no place for those who were disrespectful or demeaning. "People do not understand the pain and hurt that these words can inflict on their victims," said one university dean.[32] And, as they had with the creationists, fair-minded people had to admit that the humanitarians were on to something. The humanitarians had discovered what liberals rarely realize and almost never admit: the liberal intellectual system, whatever else it may be, is not "nice."

Somehow the idea has grown up that "liberal" means "nice," that the liberal intellectual system fosters sensitivity, toleration, self-esteem, the rejection of prejudice and bias. That impression is misguided. The truth is that liberal science demands discipline as well as license, and to those who reject or flout its rules, it can be cruel. It excludes and restricts as well as tolerates. It thrives on prejudice no less than on cool detachment. It does not give a damn about your feelings and happily tramples them in the name of finding truth. It allows and—here we should be honest—sometimes encourages offense. Self-esteem, sensitivity, respect for others' beliefs, renunciation of prejudice are all good as far as they go. But as primary social goals they are incompatible with the peaceful and productive advancement of human knowledge. To advance knowledge, we must all sometimes suffer. Worse than that, we must inflict suffering on others.

Just as the losers in the game of science—creationists, Afrocentrists, and so on—had risen up and demanded inclusion, so did the offended demand redress and an end to the hurting. The time had come, they said, to reconsider the liberal-science system, to retreat from it or revise it or put sensible and humane controls on it—perhaps even to junk it.

Then came a defining moment, though to this day it has not, I believe, been properly recognized as such. All at once lightning illuminated a garish landscape which until then had been seen only in patches here and there. In February 1989, fundamentalist Muslims rose up against the British writer Salman Rushdie, who had written a novel which they regarded as deeply, shockingly, offensive to Islam's holy truths and to the Muslim community. As they understood it, the novel implied that Muhammad had made up the Koran, an outrageous (to them) slander against their holy book's divine origin. The novel fantasized about a whorehouse where each whore takes on the name, even the personality, of one of Muhammad's wives. It suggested that Muhammad might have bent his divine inspirations to suit his political needs or even his convenience. It referred to him as "Mahound." That was what they saw.

The Ayatollah Ruhollah Khomeini proclaimed that it was the duty of all good Muslims to kill Salman Rushdie: "It is incumbent on every Muslim to employ everything he has got, his life and his wealth, to send him to hell." Rushdie went underground. "I feel as if I have been plunged, like Alice, into the world beyond the looking glass," he wrote a year later, "where nonsense is the only available sense. And I wonder if I'll ever be able to climb back through."[33]

Happening as it did in the year when communism crumbled, the Rushdie affair flashed into headlines but then sank into history. It soon became a historical footnote, partly because Khomeini himself died soon afterwards. And the attack itself was not so very surprising; fundamentalists have made a hobby of harassing the unorthodox for centuries. The surprise was that the reply from the liberal democracies was muttered and utterly incoherent. A long week of silence passed before President George Bush got around to saying, unimpressively, that the death decree was "deeply offensive." The Japanese government said, "Mentioning and encouraging murder is not something to be praised."

In the end the Rushdie affair showed us graphically two things, one which we knew already and one which we did not know at all. What we knew already was that fundamentalism—not just religious fundamentalism, but any fundamentalist system for settling differences of opinion—is the enemy of free thought. More frightening was what we had not known: Western intellectuals did not have a clear answer, many had no answer at all, to the challenge that Khomeini set before them.

That challenge was at least twofold. First, it was a restatement of the creationists' challenge, the angry outsiders' cry from the heart: Who gave you, the arrogant West, the right to make the rules? You are imperialists with your view of truth, with your insistence on the intellectual ways of secularism and of science. How dare you flout and mock our view of truth?

The point was noted at the time. What was not so widely noted was the second dimension of Khomeini's challenge: the humanitarian dimension. This is not to say that Khomeini was a humanitarian, only that the argument which his supporters commonly made was humanitarian in principle: "You have *hurt* us with your evil words, your impious words, disrespectfully and needlessly written in utter disregard of Muslim sensibilities. You have caused pain and offense to many people. And this you have no right to do."

We liberals will never be able to answer those complaints honestly or consistently until we grit our teeth and admit the truth. Yes, Rushdie's words caused many people anger and pain. *And that is all right.* But no such honest admission, and therefore no clear defense, was forthcoming. People often did not seem even to know what it was—free speech? religious liberty? nonviolence? respect for other cultures?—that they were defending. They certainly seemed not to understand the principles upon which the liberal intellectual system is based. A lot of people seemed to have the impression that the Western intellectual system is a kind of anything-goes pluralism in which all ways of believing are created equal and the only rule is "Be nice." "Well," quite a few people said apologetically at the time of the Rushdie incident, "for Khomeini to have ordered Rushdie's death was of course bad, and he shouldn't have done that, but Rushdie certainly did write a book which was offensive to Islamic truths, and he shouldn't have done that, either." The chief rabbi of Great Britain said that the book should not have been published. "Both Mr. Rushdie and the Ayatollah have abused freedom of speech."[34]

That was the sense in which the Rushdie affair was a defining moment. It showed how readily Westerners could be backed away from a fundamental principle of intellectual liberalism, namely that there is nothing whatever wrong with offending—hurting people's feelings—in pursuit of truth. That principle seemed to have been displaced by a belief in the right not to be offended, which was quickly gaining currency in America. At Harvard in 1989, about the same time as the Rushdie affair, a professor of ichthyology reportedly said at a panel discussion on race relations that in a lecture one should never "introduce any sort of thing that might hurt a group." He said, "The pain that racial insensitivity can create is more important than a professor's academic freedom."[35]

You can hear that sort of thing on campuses across America nowadays, and echoes of it in the newspapers and practically everywhere else. America is full of people who deplored Khomeini's attack on Rushdie but launched similar, if less deadly, attacks on "offensive" persons here at home. On the first anniversary of the death sentence, Rushdie, from his hiding place, published an article in which he said that, without the freedom to offend, freedom of expression ceases to exist.[36] That very same week, the columnist and television commentator Andy Rooney, to save his job, found himself apologizing for a statement which he denied ever having made. (He had been quoted as saying that "most people are born with equal intelligence, but blacks have watered down their genes because the less intelligent ones are the ones that have the most children. They drop out of school early, do drugs, and get pregnant.") Rooney got off with a suspension from his job at CBS News after offering "his deepest apologies to any in our society who were given offense."

CBS was legally entitled to suspend its commentators for allegedly making statements which offended people, for having white hair, or even for being embarrassingly banal. What was disturbing was not the legality of CBS's action but the mentality which seemed to impel it: the activists' belief that they had a right not to be offended, and the network's readiness to concede that right. Meanwhile, where were other commentators who may someday also be accused of offending? "Call [it] censorship if you like," wrote Walter Goodman of the *New York Times*, assessing CBS's action. "American television lives by that sort of censorship and so makes a considerable contribution to the country. . . . And whatever the justice of his punishment, [Rooney] can take comfort in having served as a sacrifice to the cause of public tranquillity."[37] As for Rooney, he seemed to have learned his lesson. He decided to kill a critical commentary on black colleges. "I just decided it was so touchy I'd better not do it," he said. "In view of my problems, I decided not to push it."[38]

Every day brings new reports of thought vigilantism—citizen posses organized to punish people with wrong and dangerous ideas. In December 1990 the *Philadelphia Inquirer* ran an editorial suggesting as a possibility (though not advocating) that welfare mothers be offered incentives to use a contraceptive implant. ("No one should be compelled.") People immediately rose up to denounce the editorial as racist; to have even raised the idea was insensitive. The paper, feeling obliged to redress the "pain and suffering" caused by the editorial, soon followed with another editorial, headlined "An Apology: The Editorial on 'Norplant and Poverty' Was Misguided and Wrong-Headed." At about the same time, Puerto Rican activists took up the cause of getting Carlos Alberto Montaner fired. He was a Cuban-American TV commentator who was asked on the air why Puerto Ricans in the United States suffer worse economic conditions than other Hispanic groups. He replied, "There's probably more than one explanation, but the one that seems the most important to me is this: because there is a grave family problem in the Puerto Rican ghettos of the United States, where there are thousands of single mothers, very young, who try to escape poverty through welfare or through new partners who then leave, and leave behind other children to worsen the problem." When the uproar—"sexism," "stereotypes," and the like—began, he apologized, but (reported the *New York*

Times) "a coalition of 25 Puerto Rican organizations in New York City that has led efforts to have Mr. Montaner dismissed said yesterday that it was not appeased." The spokesman for a company that joined a boycott designed to get Montaner fired said: "His comments were an insult to the Puerto Rican community. Freedom of speech is not the right to insult a community."[39]

Those words—"Freedom of speech is not the right to insult a community"—could have come straight from the mouths of the Muslims who demanded that the hurtful, insulting Rushdie be punished. It is important to see that Khomeini, the angry Puerto Ricans, the college anti-bigotry activists, and all the others were acting, not just desultorily and emotionally, but consistently and in the cause of a principle: that you are not entitled to hurt me or others with words or ideas. You should not inflict pain and suffering on others with ideas and talk any more than with clubs and knives.

That principle has caught on fast. It has, indeed, begun to shape the law. Recent years have seen the rapid rise of what have become known as hate-crime statutes, which typically create special criminal offenses or require special sentences for crimes committed "with specific intent to intimidate or harass another person because of that person's race, color, religion, gender, or national origin." (The language is from Michigan's ethnic intimidation law and is more or less typical.) Well over half the states in the union, and many localities, have such laws. The hate-crimes approach (as distinct from the hate-*speech* approach) says that the expression of prejudice or bigotry by itself should not be punished, but the expression of prejudice accompanied by violence or vandalism should be.

The constitutionality of such laws is a subject of hot debate; in June 1992 the U.S. Supreme Court cast a pall over hate-crime laws by overturning a particularly broad St. Paul, Minnesota, ordinance that criminalized bigoted insults and symbols. But the *idea* behind the laws also needs debating: that a prosecutor or politician can put his finger on particularly hurtful words and ideas and, when they are accompanied by other crimes, punish people for expressing or even thinking them.

In the U.S. Congress in 1992, a bill was introduced "to provide sentencing enhancements" (in English, harsher penalties) for crimes "in which the defendant's conduct was motivated by hatred, bias, or prejudice." Such a law could not be enforced without putting the defendant's opinions on trial. (What was he thinking about blacks at the time of the crime? What does he think about them generally? Is that a "prejudice"?) Ohio passed an ethnic intimidation law that deemed crimes more serious if committed "by reason of the race, color, religion, or national origin of another person or group of persons." That verged on making what a defendant said or believed about race a part of the criminal charge (and, as a state appellate court pointed out in overturning the law, it "vests virtual[ly] complete discretion in the hands of the state to determine whether a suspect committed the alleged acts based on . . . race, color, religion, or national origin"). St. Paul's ordinance—the one that the Supreme Court struck down—went a step further by making it a misdemeanor to place "on public *or private* property a symbol, object, appellation, characterization, or graffiti, including but not limited to a burning cross or a Nazi swastika, which one knows or has reasonable grounds to know arouses anger, alarm, or resentment in others on the basis of race, color, creed, or religion" (italics added). The ordinance seemed to say that it was a hate crime to upset someone. In Florida a black man was charged under the state's hate-crime law for calling a white policeman a "cracker." In Massachusetts state legislators tried to make it a "crime against humanity" to satirize or modernize religious figures and texts.[40] (Those legislators might have been interested to know that in Pakistan thirty-year-old Tahir Iqbal was languishing in Lahore's Kot Lakhpat jail, "accused of having made 'insulting remarks against the religion of Islam' and defiling the Koran—'as a result of which the religious feelings of Muslims were wounded.' ")[41] In all of those cases, the underlying ethical principle was the same: that people who cause grave offense have committed a kind of crime. True, many people, not least of them the justices on the Supreme Court, questioned whether the American government could constitutionally punish such crimes. Yet few seemed to question whether, as a moral matter, the crime existed.

Today a new ethical concept has been established, one with extraordinary implications. It is the notion of "verbal harassment," "words that wound," "assaultive speech." Hurtful words are a kind of violence, that notion holds. It is, of course, a form of the Humanitarian Principle mentioned above. And it is immediately appealing in a way that liberal science is not. Its strong moral traction tugs at anyone who cares about others, and it has a wonderful moral clarity: Thou shalt not hurt others with words. That precept looks harmless, even admirable. Yet as the concern not to offend ascended the ethical scale from good manners to social imperative, a long-familiar side effect was ascending with it, like a childhood nightmare returning to haunt the adult: if hurting people with words is wrong, then the people who commit the offense must be called to account. And called to account they were—by offended activists and sympathetic authorities in France, in Canada, in American universities. "Only when insults, harassment, disrespect and obscenity are banned [in universities] can people engage in truly substantive argument," wrote a syndicated columnist and a prominent scientist in the *New York Times*.[42] Intellectual authoritarianism, so long disgraced, was returning to favor—this time not among religious reactionaries or fringe radicals or cultural primitives or McCarthyite paranoiacs, but among Western educated elites. Opposition to unfettered criticism was now arising from within criticism's core constituency. Intellectuals' ranks were deeply divided, and the humanitarians who called for bans on "insults, harassment, disrespect and obscenity" had seized the moral offensive.

And this is where our two stories converge. From modest beginnings with creationists and bluenoses have grown two full-fledged and linked challenges to the legitimacy of liberal science. Taken together, they are the most conceptually cogent and far-reaching challenges since the days of the great battles between science and religion. One challenge says that the liberal intellectual system is unfair, the other that it is hurtful, both that it must therefore be regulated. Exclusion is unfair—exclusion of creationism from biology classes, of Afrocentrism from history classes, of Christian Science from medical respectability. Therefore exclusion should be stopped.

And offensive words and ideas hurt. Therefore they also should be stopped.

Of the two, the humanitarian challenge is the more dangerous. We will pay a heavy price if the principle takes root in our ethical code that the offended, having been hurt, have the right to an apology and to redress. It is crucial to understand that the Humanitarian Principle is deadly—inherently deadly, not incidentally so—to intellectual freedom and to the productive and peaceful pursuit of knowledge. The principle takes aim not just at freedom of speech but at *liberal science itself*. It is equally deadly whether espoused by Islamic fundamentalists ("Rushdie owes Muslims an apology"), by Christians, or by minority activists ("Andy Rooney owes an apology to 'any in our society who were given offense' "). It leads to the doctrine that people should be punished for holding false or dangerous beliefs. It leads, in other words, toward an inquisition.

I hope to show that the humanitarians' and egalitarians' claim to the moral high ground is false and that intellectual liberalism, with its commitment to allow and even sometimes encourage offense, is the only genuinely humane system. I hope to show that people who are "hurt by words" are morally entitled to nothing whatsoever by way of compensation. What is the right answer to the person who demands something because he is offended? Just this: "Too bad, but you'll live." As for people who call for punishment of "racists," "homophobes," "sexists," "blasphemers," "Communists," or whoever the bogeyman happens to be—those people are enemies of inquiry and their clamor deserves only to be ignored, never humored.

More specifically, this book will try to establish the following points. First, there are not two great liberal social and political systems but three. One is democracy—political liberalism—by which we decide who is entitled to use force; another is capitalism—economic liberalism—by which we decide how to allocate resources. The third is liberal science, by which we decide who is right.

Second, the third system has been astoundingly successful, not merely as a producer of technology but also, far more important, as a peacemaker and builder of social bridges. Its great advantages as a social system for raising and settling differences of opinion are inherent, not incidental. However, its disadvantages—it causes pain and suffering, it creates legions of losers and outsiders, it is disorienting and unsettling, it allows and even thrives on prejudice and bias—are also inherent. And today it is once again under attack.

Third, the attackers seek to undermine the two social rules which make liberal science possible. (I'll outline them in the next chapter and elaborate them in the rest of the book.) For the system to function, people must try to follow those rules even if they would prefer not to. Unfortunately, many people are forgetting them, ignoring them, or carving out exemptions.

That trend must be fought, because, fourth, the alternatives to liberal science lead straight to authoritarianism. And intellectual authoritarianism, although once the province of the religious and the political right in America, is now flourishing among the secular and the political left.

Fifth, behind the new authoritarian push are three idealistic impulses: Fundamentalists want to protect the truth. Egalitarians want to help the oppressed and let in the excluded. Humanitarians want to stop verbal violence and the pain it causes. The three impulses are now working in concert.

Sixth, fundamentalism, properly understood, is not about religion. It is about the inability to seriously entertain the possibility that one might be wrong. In individuals such fundamentalism is natural and, within reason, desirable. But when it becomes the foundation for an intellectual system, it is inherently a threat to freedom of thought.

Seventh, there is no way to advance knowledge peacefully and productively by adhering to the principles advocated by egalitarians and humanitarians. Their principles are poisonous to liberal science and ultimately to peace and freedom.

Eighth, no social principle in the world is more foolish and dangerous than the rapidly rising notion that hurtful words and ideas are a form of violence or torture (e.g., "harassment") and that their perpetrators should be treated accordingly. That notion leads to the criminalization of criticism and the empowerment of authorities to regulate it. The new sensitivity is the old authoritarianism in disguise, and it is just as noxious.

A brief sketch of the argument: The next chapter is about the rise of the two social rules which supplanted intellectual authoritarianism and which define liberal science. The whole of this book is an attempt to explain and defend those two rules and to make clear the obligations they impose. The third chapter explains why liberal science is unique: it uses intellectual resources efficiently, it settles differences of opinion peacefully, and it inherently blocks the political manipulation of knowledge. The fourth chapter examines the oldest of the threats to this system, that of the Fundamentalist Principle. The fifth chapter turns to the new egalitarian and humanitarian threats and shows how they lead to authoritarianism and an inquisition mentality. The sixth chapter suggests what we should do.

A final word of introduction: The one argument which you hear with any frequency in defense of liberal science is that science works. It makes airplanes and drugs and computers and dishwashers and many other good things. That is certainly true. But the argument from technology is inadequate to meet the new challenges. If we rest our case for liberal intellectual values on technology, then we wind up in an argument with people who insist that teaching Genesis 1:27 as a credible alternative to Darwin, or teaching that ancient Egyptians had black skin, will not have much effect one way or the other on mankind's ability to make airplanes and drugs. Some very good engineers and researchers happen to be creationists, and it does them no harm. You do not necessarily have to accept liberal intellectual values in order to run a computer-chip design lab—so the argument goes. The Soviet Union proved that you can stifle liberal inquiry and still have a high-tech space program. In fact, the Ayatollah Khomeini himself argued for technology without liberalism. The televisions and airplanes which he depended on, it was pointed out to him, were the products of the West. Yes, he said, "these are the good things from the West. And we are not afraid to use them, and we do. We are not afraid of your science and of your technology. We are afraid of your ideas and of your customs. Which means that we fear you politically and socially."[43]

Liberal science is not, finally, a way of making things. It is a way of organizing society and a way of behaving. To defend it by pointing just to its technological success is to defend the laboratories while abandoning the social infrastructure that makes them work. In any case, most of what modern intellectuals do does not make technology; it makes knowledge. Sociology and economics do not cure cancer, nor are they much good at making predictions—but they, no less than physics and chemistry, deserve to be defended against people who want to tinker with their results or regulate them for political reasons.

This essay proposes a more fundamental, and more radical, kind of answer to the enemies of criticism. It requires thinking of science in a way which at first may seem strange—in a very broad way, and particularly in a political way. It requires thinking about science as a set of rules for social behavior, rules for settling conflict. To think that way means, to begin with, understanding what the rules of the game are, and how philosophers like Descartes and Hume launched a social revolution no less than a philosophical one.

2

The Rise of Liberal Science

In the beginning was Plato, the greatest of all the masters who have advocated centralized control of knowledge. His unresting spirit continues to haunt us; it probably always will. No one has ever made the Fundamentalist Principle for knowledge-making so dazzling, so compelling, so beautiful. No one has more sublimely argued that opinion must be regulated for the good of society.

There are many reasons to read Plato, among them the beauty and plasticity of his thought and the delightful character of Socrates, but surely one of the best reasons to read him is to be horrified. Read *The Republic,* putative wellspring of Western values, and you find that once you look past the glittering facade of Plato's rhetoric you are face to face with the ethic of the totalitarian regime. It was that Republic of Plato's which John Locke, David Hume, and the other founding fathers of the liberal epistemological regime rebelled against and, eventually, overthrew. But though they put the Platonic Republic on the defensive, they did not extinguish the life in it. Plato's shining vision is immediately appealing, and you have to think hard about it to see why it is bad. It holds out the promise of governance by the enlightened and humane, of relief from the foolish and unreasonable, of shelter from uncertainty and change. Today, as ever, it is a magnet drawing millions of people, including many American intellectuals, toward the political regulation of inquiry.

In fairness, the dark Plato was not the only one. Like all of us, he had more than one side, and there isn't a soul who doesn't find much to love in him. Every liberal loves the figure of Socrates, who has taught so many people the method of skeptical inquiry and the importance of intellectual humility—of trying to keep in mind the difference between what you know and what you just *think* you know. Plato loved Socrates too; and it is, for me, as a philosopher of love that Plato achieves his most moving art. He was a rhetorician capable of Mozartean fertility and lyricism; he was capable, too, of irony, of doubling back to undermine himself, of leading himself astray as though to sow discontent with his own glibness. To academics and others who have spent their working lives with him, I ought to say that I have no intention of encapsulating Plato in the few pages that follow. I mean only to follow one of the particularly important strands in the tapestry, a political strand woven primarily into *The Republic*.

Plato's ideal Republic, his vision of the good political regime, is built on the following principles.

The founding principle is that of absolute individual devotion to, and submission to, the good of the state. The state should control procreation and marriage, for eugenic and population-control purposes, so as to prevent the racial debasement of the ruling (guardian) class. To keep the genetic stock strong, "the offspring of the inferior and any of those of the other sort who are born defective" should be "properly dispose[d] of in secret, so that no one will know what has become of them" (460c).[1] The private family should be abolished among the ruling class and children raised collectively, so that "these women shall all be common to all these men, and that none shall cohabit with any privately, and that the children shall be common, and that no parent shall know its own offspring nor any child its parent" (457d). Similarly, private property should be abolished among the ruling class as a way to get rid of the very notion of a private or individual interest, "so that we can count on their being free from the dissensions that arise among men from the possession of property, children, and kin" (464e).

The state cannot inculcate the necessary beliefs and virtues in its administrative class unless it exercises strict and vigilant control of speech, including poetry. "We must begin, then, it seems, by a censorship over our story-makers" (377c). Music, too, is corrupting if unsupervised. Not even Homer himself is to be spared. "We will beg Homer and the other poets not to be angry if we cancel those and all similar passages," says Plato, after citing verses of the kind which "we will expunge" (387b and 386c). Still he is not finished: all artisans, all artists, all craftsmen are to be carefully watched by the overseers, "on penalty, if unable to obey, of being forbidden to practice their art among us, that our guardians may not be bred among symbols of evil" (401b). No form of expression, in short, is to be untouched by the state's tendrils. Lest corruption creep in, the state "must throughout be watchful against innovations in music and gymnastics counter to the established order" (424b). Just so did Stalin and his minions supervise the innovations of Shostakovich.

Supporting the whole regime, and giving it legitimacy, is "one noble lie" told among the ruling elite. The rulers, in their turn, will administer a regimen of propaganda lies to keep the social structure stable: "our rulers will have to make considerable use of falsehood and deception for the benefit of their subjects" (459c). A ruler may lie as necessary, but, just as you might expect, if he "catches anybody else in the city lying . . . he will chastise him for introducing a practice as subversive and destructive of a state as it is of a ship" (389d). At the top, ruling over all, is the wise philosopher, whose love of wisdom "is impossible for the multitude" (494a). The philosopher-rulers are very great indeed, virtually gods, and when they die "the state shall establish public memorials and sacrifices for them" (540c). There might be posters staring down from high places to remind ordinary people of their former leaders' omniscience; there might be a grand mausoleum in the Republic's main square, and monumental idealized statues in all provinces.

What makes the whole massive totalitarian machine possible is the view of knowledge which undergirds it. Plato believed what so many of us instinctively believe: that the way to produce knowledge is to sit down in a quiet spot and think clearly. The best knowledge comes to him who thinks best. Liberalism holds that knowledge comes only from a public process of critical exchange, in which the wise and unwise alike participate. But Plato believed that knowledge comes from wisdom, and so knowledge belongs especially to the especially wise—to the true philosophers, who are rare indeed. The real philoso-phers are the people "who are capable of apprehending that which is eternal and unchanging, while those who are incapable of this, but lose themselves and wander amid the multiplicities of multifarious things, are not philosophers" (484b). People with that nearly divine capability may approach an understanding of reality as it is, whereas others walk as though in a "dream state." Most of us live in a dim cave below ground, apprehending images only, but the philosopher can aspire to the brilliant sunshine of genuine knowledge.

Once you grant Plato his premises about knowledge, then it is clear who should rule the state and sort true opinions from false ones: the philosophers. "To them by their very nature belong the study of philosophy and political leadership, while it befits the other sort to let philosophy alone and follow their leadership" (474c). Only to those who are capable of right knowledge should truth and power be entrusted. Few people are endowed with such a capability, though many might aspire. Philosophy "is impossible for the multitude," and "the perfect philosopher is a rare growth among men and is found in only a few" (494a and 491b). Such a person, who everywhere is "seeking the true nature of everything as a whole, never sinking to what lies close at hand," is bound to be aloof and sometimes to be laughed at by "the whole rabble."[2] Never mind: here is the man whose spirit and mind are fit to rule.

And what about the "motley horde" of people who want to rule but lack the philosopher's access to knowledge? Such persons are bound to be a problem. Unless, says Plato, they are "compulsorily excluded [from power], there can be no cessation of troubles" (473d). There must be no Salman Rushdie in Plato's Republic. If such a person were somehow to survive the state-controlled education with his ambitions intact, he would have to be eliminated.

Epistemology—one's view of who can have knowledge and when—is politics, and it has the profoundest practical consequences. No better illustration exists than Plato's ghastly state, with its central control of everything, founded on central control of truth. And Plato's ideas are neither farfetched nor archaic. They are similar to the ideas undergirding, for example, the intellectual regime of Khomeini's Iran, a dictatorship of the wise.

In this chapter I want to describe the skeptical revolution which uprooted and inverted Plato's Republic and its Fundamentalist Principle. (Why I call it "fundamentalist" is left for chapter 4.) I also

want to sketch the liberal—and breathtakingly radical—truth-finding
regime which replaced Plato's authoritarianism, the better to understand how to defend the liberal regime against today's authoritarian
revival. But let me first take up a basic question which makes a good
starting point: Why did Plato—why would anyone—feel it necessary
to regulate and control knowledge so radically and overbearingly?
Why bother? What was the threat which so alarmed Plato?

If you want to clear the room at a cocktail party, say "epistemology."
People will think you are either stuttering or crazy. In college philosophy courses many of us do learn something of epistemology—usually
beginning with Plato's discussions of knowledge and ranging through
Descartes, Berkeley, and the others. But the subject is usually taught
as though the philosophy of knowledge were a game played by
intellectuals over purely abstract counters like "insensible qualities"
and "material extension" and "sense data." It's safe to say that most
of us think of epistemology, if we ever think of it at all, as the
intellectual playground of the odd.

Plato knew better. The subject of epistemology is the nature and
limits of human knowledge. Or, as Senator Howard Baker did not
quite ask during the Watergate hearings, "What can one know and
when can one know it?" The problem of what knowledge is and how
to find it is, of course, a serious question for philosophers, who for
centuries have been debating just what we are entitled to claim we
know—though unfortunately most people have trouble understanding what the philosophers are saying. However, the problem of knowledge is not, or at least should not be, a problem for philosophers
only. It enfolds one of the few really fundamental problems that any
human society must cope with if it is to survive.

Within the question of what knowledge is and how it can be
had, another question is coiled: *Who*, if anyone, can claim to have
knowledge, and under what circumstances? When is it legitimate for
me to say "I'm right and you're wrong!" and to act accordingly? This

is the problem which Plato was grappling with in *The Republic* and elsewhere: in a world of differing opinions, how do you sort truth from error? In other words, *how do you decide who is right?* It is not just that our opinions differ and that we draw different conclusions about what we see. We *see* differently. Our points of view are different, literally and figuratively. By definition, no two of us share exactly the same experiences. We all believe—taking this on faith—that there must be, "out there," an objective reality of the world as it *really* is, independent of the vagaries of human perception and misperception, a world that we would all see identically if we could all see perfectly. Philosophers have referred to that believed-in world as the external world, the objective world, the world-in-itself. I think of it as the World Out There. Plato referred to it as the world of "forms," of pure and perfect things as they eternally and really are, "the very things themselves" (479e). Plato's philosopher was the one who could aspire to know things as they really were, and so would attain definitive knowledge rather than flighty opinion. And indeed, though the World Out There may or may not actually exist, it is what we all aspire to know.

Yet the social fact is that we live in a world not of agreement but of discord, of perceived realities as multitudinous as people. Some people—George Darden's constituents—see creatures apparently from outer space. Some people believe they have seen Elvis since he died in 1977, and not all of those people are easy to dismiss as wackos. The experience of Hilda Weaver, a professional clinical psychologist, is so striking as to be worth quoting at length.

> Now, you have to realize, I have no interest in things like ghosts or ESP. I had always been very narrow-minded about the human mind. I thought that stuff was all imagination or suggestibility.
>
> This is what happened. I was in my office one evening, writing an article for a professional journal, and I looked up and Elvis Presley was sitting across from me, in the comfortable tan chair where my clients usually sit. As I realized who he was and sensed the overwhelming kindness that just lingered in the atmosphere around the man, I could tell that he thought that all was not well with me. . . .

He began to talk with me, to communicate. He said, "Are you
satisfied with your life, Missy?" That question seemed to go to the
very center of me, and I said, "You're a better psychologist than
I am, and you've never been to school." As soon as I made that
remark I felt embarrassed and ashamed of myself, as though I had
been condescending. But he smiled, and instead of being awkward,
he was completely warm and in tune. He said, "I've been to the
best school." And from the way he said it, I knew immediately he
was right. After all, he had *died*, for heaven's sake! What was I
doing feeling so smart just because there was a piece of paper on
my wall? I suddenly realized that I was in a realm where my Ph.D.
was no longer a very good credential. In the past when someone
was in that chair, I was the Ph.D. and could use that as a way to
hide, to keep from facing myself. . . .

I began to cry, from deep within myself, and he understood
immediately and he said, "Hilda, you must open up your perspective on what you are doing with your life." Then we conversed
for a while. Much of it was very personal, stuff that I'm not yet
comfortable sharing with anyone else. And by the time it was over,
I understood that there is much more to the mind and the human
spirit than I had previously allowed, and that if I was going to be
a full human being and be helpful to others, I had to realize this
and let it affect me fully. I instinctively bowed my head and put
my hands together, as in prayer. When I looked up again, he was
gone.[3]

What did she conclude? That Elvis was alive? That he was dead
but that death isn't really final? That she was dreaming? That she
was mad? That is her problem, of course, but it is not only hers.
What are the rest of us supposed to say? Most of us would probably
say that she was deluded or hallucinating or dreaming. But how do
we know? Wouldn't it be fairer to say that Elvis might or might not
be dead? Should the Internal Revenue Service go looking for Elvis
in order to collect back taxes? One way or another, every society
must have some prevailing standard for distinguishing between reality
and illusion, between objective knowledge and personal belief. Just
what standard is used matters enormously to somebody like Hilda
Weaver, a clinical psychologist whose reputation and, indeed, sanity
are on the line.

Moreover, the standard chosen has profound political implications. Any attempt to decide who is right will inevitably make some people winners and others losers. So we arrive back at the creationist question: what gives the pro-science people the right to declare themselves the winners?

And we arrive, also, at the problem that Plato was up against. Diversity, of belief, thought, opinion, experience, is a fact, like it or not. Harness it, and you have the engine that generates knowledge. But diversity of belief is also a dangerous social problem, because it makes conflict inevitable. How do you stop people from breaking up into little tribes, each with its own opinion, or from fighting each other to decide who is right? Differences of opinion can bring people to blows and push countries toward hostilities. ("More Japanese Deny Nation Was Aggressor During World War II; Spread of Revisionist View Irks Many Other Asians.")[4] Moreover, Plato believed that a good and stable society must base its decisions upon correct information and truthful principles; but, in a world abuzz with conflicting opinion, most people will necessarily not know or believe the truth. In fact, most of the time most people will be wrong, some of them dangerously so. What if *they* come to power? How do you ensure that truth prevails, and what do you do about the people who are not inclined to believe it? How do you bring countless millions of subjective realities to some kind of convergence? And if you cannot, whom do you believe?

How to manage conflict of belief is, I submit, a problem that every society must somehow solve. Upon the solution chosen depends, not only social peace and cohesion, but also the structure of our most important industry: the reality industry.

That industry is charged with producing true statements about the external world. Its mission is to tell us how things "really" are. Its millions of professionals work in laboratories and schools and think tanks and newsrooms all over the world. As a journalist, I happen to be a worker in the knowledge industry; the same can be said of most intellectuals, whether they are chemists or literary critics.

It always amazes me to see how little attention we pay to the knowledge-making business. I spend a lot of my time writing on

economic policy issues, and I spend a lot of *that* time simply trying
not to drown under the tide of papers and studies and newsletters
and articles and books and speeches and programs and policies which
wash across my desk and then on into oblivion. From Wall Street,
from universities, from the government, from journalists—on and on
they come. Capitalism, socialism, free trade, managed trade, planning,
laissez faire—we are obsessed with debating how society ought to
organize itself to create material product. We talk ceaselessly about
questions like, Who (government, private sector, other) should decide
what is the right level of investment or the ideal balance of trade?
But we ignore questions like, Who should decide what kind of questions to ask, what kind of research to do? The imbalance is bizarre.
True, we build fine buildings and invent prodigious machines and
pile up dazzling wealth. But the greatest of all human products is
our knowledge.

And knowledge is a product, like the metals we mine and the cars
we build. To be more specific, our knowledge is a set of statements
which we are satisfied are true—which have been validated, truth
tested, in some satisfactory way. "The moon revolves around the
earth." "In 1492 Columbus sailed the ocean blue." And so on. This
is the product of the knowledge industry: a set of statements which
have been found worthy and which we rely on.

So far, so good. But now we come to the difficult question, the
question fudged by the passive-voice construction "which have been
found worthy." Found worthy *by whom?* Obviously, creationists and
evolutionists will have different ideas about who should test beliefs
about human creation, and how. Given that our experiences and
conclusions will be different, what will be the test of truth? And who
will administer it? There are countless decision-making strategies you
could use. You could have everyone refer to a book or text of some
kind. ("Just look it up.") You could have an every-man-for-himself
sort of arrangement. ("Truth is in the eye of the beholder.") You
could, in principle, settle disputed questions by having some specially
appointed official flip a coin. (Although that sounds strange, such
systems, suitably refined, have in fact been commonly used. Suppose
you and your neighbor are arguing over whether or not next year's

crop will be good. Imagine going to a special temple in the center
of town where a priest utters ritual words, casts a golden coin onto
a decorated pavement, and then announces what the coin has said.
That is known as an oracle.) You could simply have a taboo against
discussing questions on which people disagree. (To some extent,
every society uses that strategy: "I never discuss politics or religion.")
You could even have people vote on what is true. (Odd as that may
sound, it is what a jury does, and it turns out not to be a bad
arrangement, as far as it goes. For all legal and public purposes, if
the jury votes that the accused did not commit the crime, the accused
did not commit the crime.) You could do some of all of those things,
and many others besides. But which?

Plato, living in the intellectual hurly-burly of ancient Athens, was
hardly blind to this problem. He was well aware that the world was
a riot of often conflicting opinions, most of which were wrong. Of the
nonphilosophers, and also of most of the philosophers, he remarked,
"Such men have opinions about all things, but know nothing of the
things they opine" (479e). How could a nation full of false and
conflicting opinions be held together?

That was not all: he was offended and alarmed by the cacophony
around him, the din made by people who spoke loudly but wrongly.
He has Socrates ask, "Do you think it right to speak as having knowledge about things one does not know?"—and the answer is emphati-
cally no. For "opinions divorced from knowledge," says Plato with
disgust, "are ugly things" (506c). Woe unto the country where the
truth is drowned out by the racket of false opinions, where the citizens
"lose themselves and wander amid the multiplicities of multifarious
things," the jungles and quicksands of errors and misperceptions.

No surprise, then, that Plato set out to show how a just society
would sort truth from error. The answer he hit upon is the one which,
to many people then and now, seems the most obvious and righteous:
he who best knows the truth will choose. The philosopher could best
tell truth from falsehood and accordingly should administer the state.
By definition, his decisions would be wisest and most truthful. Conflict would be settled fairly and effectively.

Plato was no crude fundamentalist: he did not, I think, believe
that truth was obvious or immediately accessible even to the wise.

He understood that the search for knowledge is never easy and often
fails, and he took pains to warn his readers that such was the case
by ending whole dialogues inconclusively, by having Socrates say
that he has broken his head in argument "times without number,"
and by stating flat-out that (for instance) there is always "plenty of
room for doubt, when we even doubt whether we are asleep or
awake."[5] Why, then, did Plato follow the garden-variety true believers
and fundamentalists into the morass of intellectual authoritarianism?
One answer, and a fairly compelling one, is that he was a self-serving
reactionary who wanted the job of philosopher-dictator for himself.
Another interpretation, for those who are inclined to give him the
benefit of the doubt, is that he saw no other way to resolve the
difficult political problem of intellectual conflict. Plato the epistemolo-
gist understood that truth is elusive for all of us, but Plato the realist
understood that some of us can come closer to it than others. In a
conflict of opinion between Einstein and a fool, one wishes for Einstein
to prevail. And in a conflict of opinion between Einstein and a thousand fools or a million, one wishes all the more for Einstein to prevail.
Our Einsteins or Lincolns *are* one in a million, yet somehow our frail
societies must unravel one tangled problem after another. If we are
to succeed and prosper, then we are obliged to put truth-identifying
power only in the hands of our very wisest citizens. And we must
take extreme precautions to defend their power against less wise
usurpers.

"One man is wiser than another and . . . the wiser man is the
measure," Plato says.[6] To each, then, according to his wisdom: appoint
the extraordinary thinker as arbiter of truth. Plato's logic stood dominant for two thousand years. At last it was upended by an innovation
in social thinking which audaciously replaced extraordinary philosophers with ordinary critics—an innovation whose radicalism and
brilliance were unsurpassed even by the inversions which replaced
monarchs with electorates and feudal lords with entrepreneurs.

In the first half of the seventeenth century, when René Descartes
set sail on the weird seas of philosophical skepticism, his project was

radical in the truest sense of the word. "I shall proceed by setting aside all that admits of even the very slightest doubt, just as if I had convicted it of being absolutely false," he wrote in his *Meditations* of 1641. He would peel away layers of possible deception until he arrived at one indubitable truth, which he would use as the base for a vaccine with which to kill a skeptical virus that was rampant in Europe.[7]

One way to react to widespread disagreement is the way Plato reacted: by calling for the establishment of a rightful authority to settle conflicts. But that is not the only way. Another is to throw up your hands and say: "I don't know and neither does anyone else. They're all a bunch of arrogant jabberers." In Washington, D.C., for instance, it's common to meet people who take a they're-all-full-of-it attitude in response to the endless inconclusive bickering of economists and public-policy experts. That is a skeptical reaction.

Skeptical doubters have been around since at least the days of Socrates himself and of Pyrrho of Elis (fourth century B.C.), who is supposed to have made it his aim to withhold judgment on all matters on which there were conflicting views, including the matter of whether anything was known. Skepticism typically flourishes in response to divisive and sometimes violent differences of opinion, as a way to short-circuit dangerous conflict. Ancient skepticism thrived in the medical community of Alexandria in reaction to the stubborn dogmatism of rival camps of doctors. In periods of consensus, skepticism simmers down, as it does also in periods when debate is quashed or circumscribed by political controls. Thus the skeptical schools of thought more or less disappeared behind the walls of the Church. But the walls were eventually broken, and intellectual crisis ensued. In the early sixteenth century Martin Luther declared that all Christians, not just the ones in authority, had the power of seeing and judging what is right or wrong in matters of faith. Well, if the Church did not have the sole authority to identify truth, and if people disagreed in their conclusions (as of course they did), just how was anyone supposed to know which beliefs were the right ones? What was the rule for separating reality from illusion? Who should be believed? As Plato had understood almost two millennia earlier, the problem of knowledge could tear society to shreds, and indeed, as Catholics and Protestants bloodied each other in battles across Europe, it did so.

No surprise, then, that at about that time the ancient skeptics were rediscovered. Amid the bickering and fighting they exerted a strong appeal.[8] Skepticism cropped up in the academies and reached a new pinnacle with Michel de Montaigne. "For this is a very true presupposition," he remarked with unconcealed exasperation, "that men are in agreement about nothing, I mean even the most gifted and ablest scholars, not even that the sky is over our head." Perhaps more brilliantly and ruthlessly than anyone before or since, Montaigne argued in 1577 that for man to attain knowledge was hopeless. Our judgment may lead us astray. "The slightest things in the world whirl it around." And further, "As for the error and uncertainty of the operations of the senses, each man can furnish himself with as many examples as he pleases, so ordinary are the mistakes and deceptions that they offer us." As for belief, in the past we have been wrong while believing we were right, and so sureness is no guarantee of anything. "Not that it is impossible that some true knowledge may dwell in us; but if it does, it does so by accident. And since by the same road, the same manner and process, errors are received into our soul, it has no way to distinguish them or to pick out truth from falsehood."[9] Montaigne's arguments were impeccable, but his escape from them was not. The only answer, he concluded, is for man to give up any hope of finding truth on his own and to rely upon God to reveal it to him. That, of course, was no answer at all, because the whole problem in the first place was how to be sure who spoke truly for God. With Montaigne's having destroyed certainty without providing anything to replace it, the condition of knowledge seemed desperate.

Here Descartes intervened. He searched until he found one proposition which was clearly beyond doubt: that he thought and thus knew he existed. He was certain of that because it was clear and distinct to him. Equally clear and distinct, and so equally certain, was his knowledge of God and of God's benevolence. A benevolent God would not deceive us. And so, we may conclude, that which is clear and distinct is not deceptive but certain. Therefore, we can and do, after all, have certain knowledge of the world.

The reasoning was ingenious, but it failed—one of the most fertile intellectual failures in all history. Descartes made a leap to which he was not entitled: his awareness of his own thinking did not give him the right to claim any certainty about God's objective existence, or about anything else apart from himself. Moreover, if the senses and the process of thinking could both, on occasion, be deceptive, then to say that a proposition is clear and distinct is no guarantee of anything. Subsequent thinkers were quick to see those problems and others. Descartes nonetheless achieved an important advance, not with his conclusion, but with his method. Systematic criticism was the key.

Thus began the skeptical revolution. Skeptical reasoners marched straight down the road opened by Descartes. At last in 1739 David Hume, the brilliant twenty-eight-year-old enfant terrible of modern philosophy, came along with his bulldozer and made a ruin of the last pillars of certainty about the external world. Induction—generalizing from past to future, from known to unknown—is nothing more than an act of faith, Hume said. He made a devastating argument: How can I know that the past is of any value at all as a guide to the future? I can answer, "Heretofore it always has been." But I cannot use *that* fact as a guide to the future without assuming what I set out to establish, namely that the past is a good guide to the future. Hume said, "We have no reason to draw any inference concerning any object beyond those of which we have had experience." Not only that: no experience which we *do* have can tell us anything directly about the world as it exists, or may exist, independent of ourselves. "Let us fix our attention out of ourselves as much as possible: Let us chase our imagination to the heavens, or to the utmost limits of the universe; we never really advance a step beyond ourselves."[10]

Knowledge has not been the same since. Hume demolished the logical underpinnings of all naive claims, and most sophisticated claims, that we can have any certain knowledge whatever of the objective world—the world as it "really" is, independent of human perception or misperception. And if we cannot have certainty, then what is to distinguish one man's belief as better than another's? As Montaigne himself had put the problem: "Either we judge absolutely, or we absolutely cannot." The skeptical crisis of Montaigne's time now seemed to have given way to an abyss still deeper than before, with two dreadful consequences: first, the replacing of old dogmas with a new and utterly negative one, namely that we cannot have any knowledge whatever; second, a consequent paralysis of all intellectual industry.

"Seemed," however, is the operative word. What was really going on was more subtle and interesting. A new social ethic was being born.

In its most peculiar and extreme philosophical form, skepticism refers to the doctrine that we have no reason to believe anything, and so should believe nothing. That, however, is on its face an unsustainable argument. Believing nothing is impossible. Even the belief that you are justified in believing nothing is a belief. And even when we refuse to conclude, we do so only against the background of other conclusions. No one could possibly be a genuinely beliefless skeptic, even in principle.

The "skepticism" upon which liberal science is based is something quite different. (To distinguish it from the kind which says that we should never conclude anything, philosophers often call it "fallibilism.") This kind of skepticism says cheerfully that we have to draw conclusions, but that we may regard none of our conclusions as being beyond any further scrutiny or change. "Go ahead and conclude whatever you want; just remember that all of your conclusions, every single one of them, may need to be corrected." This attitude does not require you to renounce knowledge. It requires you only to renounce certainty, which is not the same thing. In other words, your knowledge is always tentative and subject to correction. At the bottom of this kind of skepticism is a simple proposition: *we must all take seriously the idea that any and all of us might, at any time, be wrong.*

Taking seriously the idea that we might be wrong is not exactly a dogma. It is, rather, an intellectual style, an attitude or ethic. What is to be said for this ethic? Not much, on its face. It is not provable. There is nothing especially rational (or irrational) about it. It is not an intellectually neutral view of the world or a view that rises above faith, since it *is* a kind of faith—faith in the belief that we are all fallible. "Why, doubt itself is a decision of the widest practical reach," William James rightly said. "The coil is about us, struggle as we may. The only escape from faith is mental nullity."[11] One cannot overstress this point, although often no amount of emphasis seems to drive it home: to adopt the attitude that you can never be completely sure you are right is a decision, a positive step—not a void where commitment should be, but a *kind* of commitment (to taking seriously that one might be wrong). If you are not inclined to doubt, you never even reach skepticism—it is simply not an issue; you simply believe without asking questions.

What, then, is so important about the emergence, eventually the triumph, of the skeptical ethic? The answer is this: Hidden in the pages of the skeptical philosophers' tomes is a radical social principle. It is the principle of public criticism.

When people accept the notion that none of us is completely immune from error, they also implicitly accept that no person, no matter who he is or how strongly he believes, is above possible correction. If at any moment I can be wrong and you can be wrong and so can everybody else, all without being aware of it, then none of us can claim to have finally settled any dispute about the state of the external world. No one, therefore, is above critical scrutiny, nor is any belief.

The result is this: A society which has accepted skeptical principles will accept that *sincere criticism is always legitimate.* In other words, if any belief may be wrong, then no one can legitimately claim to have ended any discussion—ever.

In other words: **No one gets the final say.**

Another conclusion also follows. If any person may be in error, then no one can legitimately claim to be above being checked by others—ever. Moreover, if anyone may be in error, no one can legitimately claim to have any unique or personal powers to decide who is right and who is wrong.

In other words: **No one has personal authority.**

Here is a result which Socrates would have relished and which Plato—the Plato of *The Republic*—fought with every resource of his genius. Here is error enthroned as inevitable and inescapable, sitting in state above the philosopher-king no less than above the ignorant laborer or the cynical sophist. In most human societies for most of history, the search for knowledge had always been anchored by some propositions or some authorities—a Bible or other texts, priests or philosopher-kings or other persons—which were believed to be reliable and beyond error, and which therefore were not open to serious questioning. With the skeptical revolution, the anchor was sawed off. *Nothing* would be out of bounds for critical scrutiny. *No one* would be entitled to declare what was true knowledge and what was false opinion.

And here is where one might naturally think we are in trouble. If we may all be wrong, how are we ever to decide who is right? Why did the skeptical fires not leave society in disarray, unable to believe anything, as seemed to happen during the skeptical crisis of Montaigne's day? The answer is: because the fires cleared the ground for a new and extraordinarily powerful game—the game of liberal science.

We turn, then, to the revolution proper: a political revolution of the first importance. Now, when I talk about the skeptical revolution, the philosophical one of Descartes and Hume and the others is not mainly the one I mean. What Hume and the philosophers—the theorists of knowledge—were doing was radical and important. But their adventure was an outgrowth of broader changes in the intellectual climate of the day. Even as the theorists were busy showing that certain knowledge is impossible, the scientists and scholars of the Enlightenment were showing that *un*certain knowledge *is* possible.

That process was already under way ten years after Descartes died. The physicist Freeman Dyson wrote:

> The Royal Society of London in 1660 proudly took as its motto the phrase *Nullius in Verba,* meaning "No man's word shall be

final." The assertion of papal infallibility, even in questions of faith and morals having nothing to do with science, grates harshly upon a scientist's ear. We scientists are by training and temperament jealous of our freedom. We do not in principle allow any statement whatever to be immune from doubt.[12]

Liberal science is a big and complicated thing. No one could begin to describe it fully. However, with *nullius in verba* we have reached one of the two great foundation stones of the liberal intellectual system.

I contend that these peculiar rules are two of the most successful social conventions which the human species has ever evolved. Put them into effect, and you have laid the groundwork for a knowledge-producing and dispute-resolving system that beats all competitors hands down. They are the basis of liberal inquiry and of science. Everything that follows in this essay is ultimately an attempt to defend them, and the attacks of the creationists and humanitarians and others are ultimately attempts to undermine them.

First, the skeptical rule. If people follow it, then no idea, however wise and insightful its proponent, can ever have any claim to be exempt from criticism by anyone, no matter how stupid and grubby-minded the critic. The skeptical rule is,

> *No one gets the final say:* you may claim that a statement is established as knowledge only if it can be debunked, in principle, and only insofar as it withstands attempts to debunk it.

This is, more or less, what the great twentieth-century philosopher of science Karl R. Popper and his followers have called the principle of falsifiability. Science is distinctive, not because it proves true statements, but because it seeks systematically to disprove (falsify) false ones. In practice, of course, it is sometimes hard, if not impossible, to say whether a given statement is falsifiable or not. But what counts is the way the rule directs us to try to *act*. In principle, if you do not try to check ideas by trying to debunk them, then you are not practicing science. You are entitled to claim that a statement is objectively true only insofar as it is both checkable and has stood up to

checking, and not otherwise. Decisions about what is and is not true
are always provisional, standing only until debunked.

Second, the empirical rule. If people follow it in deciding who is
right and who is wrong, then no one gets special say simply on the
basis of who he happens to be. The empirical rule is,

> No one has personal authority: you may claim that a statement has
> been established as knowledge only insofar as the method used
> to check it gives the same result regardless of the identity of the
> checker, and regardless of the source of the statement.

In other words, whatever you do to check a proposition must be
something that anyone can do, at least in principle, and get the same
result. Who you are doesn't count; the rules apply to everybody,
regardless of identity. A test is valid only insofar as it works for
anyone who tries it. Where different checkers (debunkers) get different results, no one's result supersedes anyone else's, and no result
can be declared. The test remains inconclusive. (It is important to
note that "no personal authority" says nothing against expertise. It
only says that no one, expert or amateur, gets to claim special authority
simply because of who he happens to be or what he is saying. Whatever you do to become an expert must thus be something that others
also could do. You may have a Ph.D., but I could get one. The views
of experts, no less than those of laymen, are expected to withstand
checking.)

Those two rules define a decision-making system which people
can agree to use to figure out whose opinions are worth believing.
Under this system, you can do anything you wish to test a statement,
as long as you follow the rules, which effectively say:

- The system may not fix the outcome in advance or for good
(no final say).
- The system may not distinguish between participants (no personal authority).

The rules establish, if you will, a game—like chess or baseball.
And this particular game has the two distinctive characteristics that

define a *liberal* game: if you play it, you can't set the outcome in advance, and you can't exempt any player from the rules, no matter who he happens to be.

Game-playing is a good way to make touchy social decisions systematically. Suppose a group needs a leader. It could use a game with the following rules. Rule 1: each member of the group gets one vote in each round of vote-casting. Rule 2: whoever gets the least number of votes in each round of vote-casting is out of the game. Rule 3: the last remaining vote-getter is the group's legitimate leader till the next vote. Thus the liberal game of voting.

Suppose a group needs to decide which of several conflicting ideas is right. Again, a game. First, each school of thought places its opinion before the group. Second, friends and enemies of the ideas begin testing and criticizing, poking and prodding, checking and cross-checking. To check, players can do all kinds of things. Their tests can include real experiment, thought experiment, plausibility, simplicity, generality, utility, logical consistency, beauty—always understanding, however, that whatever test they use has to be a test that I or anyone else also can use, at least in principle (no personal authority). If, for you, a theory passes the test of experiment or beauty, then it must do the same for me and for others, or else the theory has not checked out conclusively. Third, everyone is entitled to modify one of the original ideas or to suggest a new one. Fourth, the opinion which emerges as the survivor is the winner—only, however, for as long as it continues to survive (no final say). Thus the liberal game of science.

Whenever you and others agree to follow those rules, there are a million things you might do to investigate reality—but whatever you do will look a lot like science. One way or another, you will wind up with a system in which anyone is entitled to check (criticize) anyone, and no one is immune from being checked by anyone else; in which people argue from the basis of statements that have checked out so far; in which people look for tests that anyone can perform, and claim a strong result only where there is strong independent agreement; and in which no one's experience or conclusion is supposed to get special weight by dint of who he happens to be.

The game of science is not just for "scientists." It encompasses the defining ethic of the whole vast culture of critical, liberal inquiry. A while ago I went to hear a foreign-relations expert in Washington talk about Soviet behavior under Gorbachev. He gave his view and then announced, "That's a hypothesis, and I would be willing to test it in discussion." He was playing the science game. Even journalists are trained to respect the liberal rules and obey them as far as possible. We are supposed to reject anybody's claims (including our own) to having the ultimate truth, and we try to learn how to write as though Everyman, a reasonable anybody, were standing in our shoes. An old newsroom dictum goes, "If someone says your mother loves you, check it." We journalists are not scientists, exactly, but we certainly try to play by the rules of the science game. When, that is, we are doing our job.

The skeptical revolution was gradual and nonviolent; it was fomented not by a few noisy activists but through the evolving everyday practices of thousands of intellectuals, moving as best they could from one decision about the world to the next. Its radicalism is thus easy to miss. Besides, science has a genius for looking sober and conservative; and in many ways, especially in the face it presents to the public (and the way it usually sees itself), it is sober and conservative. But in a deeper sense it is quite probably the most radical endeavor ever embarked on by mankind—radical in two ways.

First, it has completely abolished inerrancy. "There is nothing like absolute certainty in the whole field of our knowledge," writes Popper.[13] Before the revolution Montaigne could declare, "Either we judge absolutely, or we absolutely cannot." Afterwards, his formula stood on its head: if we judge absolutely, we absolutely do not. Knowledge must be debunkable and stands only until it is debunked. In a liberal scientific society, to claim that you are above error is the height of irresponsibility. Always we must hunt for error. Many of the best thinkers take that injunction—a moral duty, really—quite seriously. Stephen W. Hawking, the physicist, tells a charming story of how he bet that his own theory of black holes was wrong. "This is a form of insurance policy for me," he says. "I have done a lot of work on black holes, and it would all be wasted if it turned out that black holes do not exist. But in that case, I would have the consolation of winning my bet, which would bring me four years of the magazine *Private Eye*."[14] To the law of fallibility, the law of no final say, there are no exceptions. That is why liberals, whether religious or not, cringe in revulsion at the self-inflation of preachers and priest-dictators who claim certainty for their every whim. Those people have the gall to exempt themselves from the duty of fallibility. They have the gall to claim the last word and proclaim that criticism is unnecessary, as Plato did when he claimed for his philosopher special access to knowledge of the immutable truths laid up in heaven.

Radical, too, in another way—breathtakingly so. Today we take empiricism almost completely for granted. We forget that a philosopher like Plato, who held that only the wise philosopher could hope for knowledge of things as they really are, would have been horrified by our widespread acceptance of the empirical rule (no personal authority). For that rule has opened up the entirety of human knowledge to scrutiny by anyone and everyone. In principle, a beggar, a dockworker, an obscure patent examiner (Einstein, by name) could overturn the laws of Newton himself. The empirical rule has made knowledge public property and thrown the philosopher-king out the window as a fraud and a shaman.

The point bears explaining.

A lot of people think that what is unique about science is its empiricism: it relies on experience to confirm or throw out statements about reality. Of course, it does do that. But empiricism in that sense is hardly unique to science. All human beings make up their minds by referring to experience. It was the experience of seeing a light from heaven and hearing a voice ask, "Saul, Saul, why persecutest thou me?" that won Paul over to Christianity. The question which matters is not "Do you rely on experience to make up your mind about objective statements?" It is "*Whose* experience do you rely on?" This is where the empirical rule produces its unique answer: *only the experience of no one in particular.*

The empirical rule says, "You may claim that a statement has been established as knowledge only insofar as the method used to check it gives the same result regardless of the identity of the checker, and regardless of the source of the statement." In other words, in checking—deciding what is worth believing—*particular persons are interchangeable.*

Interchangeability of persons (we all play by the same rules) is a hallmark of liberal social philosophy. Kant declared that an action can be right for one person only if it is right for any and all, and so codified the liberal standard of justice. The empiricists declared that a statement can be true for one person only if it is true for any and all, and so codified the liberal standard for knowledge.

This is a point which has been missed again and again: scientific empiricism is a *social* philosophy. If the empiricists had said, "We must make our judgments by relying on experience—specifically, the experience of the pope," then they would have contributed nothing original. Pharaoh saw seven famished cows devour seven fat ones; it was by reference to that experience that he set his agricultural policy. But the experience was strictly private; it was dream experience (which, while it is happening, is of course sometimes just as real seeming as the waking kind). If Joseph had been an empiricist, he would have told Pharaoh that the dream experience, however real to Pharaoh, could not be shown to others and therefore did not count. Only public (or potentially public) experience counts.

For example, suppose Smith, Jones, and Brown all want to know what the temperature is outside. They refer to the thermometer. But suppose the thermometer they refer to is strange. Smith looks at it and gets a reading of 76 degrees; Jones gets a reading of 31 degrees; Brown gets 103. One approach would be for each to claim he had the right answer and regard the other two as fools—an eminently human solution. But if they follow the empirical rule (the test must give the same result regardless of the identity of the tester), they will scratch their heads and go off in search of a better test. In fact, they will probably conclude that the "thermometer" was actually telling them something about themselves, much as a blood-pressure gauge might, rather than about the world outside themselves.

This is not just an academic exercise. Think about the woman who met Elvis. A friend of mine says his mother saw Jesus descend amid a shower of golden light in the Dome of the Rock in Jerusalem. Another of my friends saw an enormous, cigar-shaped UFO hover low above the trees one night and then zip away at hyperspeed. On August 16, 1988, the *Houston Chronicle* reported:

> LUBBOCK—Worshipers screamed and lifted their hands toward the sky as a ray of light burst through the clouds Monday night during an outdoor Mass where thousands came expecting a miracle.
>
> Shortly after the 6 p.m. Mass began at St. John Neumann Catholic Church, throngs of pilgrims stood and applauded as many spectators pointed skyward, crying that they saw Jesus and the Virgin Mary, and calling it a miracle.
>
> "I saw the sun pulsating a lot and saw Jesus about 10 times," said Mamie Fertitta. "Then I saw Jesus above and the doves below."
>
> A dozen priests standing on a rooftop altar and 600 Eucharist ministers turned their backs to the crowd to look at the sky and wave. After minutes of silence, St. John Neumann pastor Monsignor Joseph James began to sing *Amazing Grace*.
>
> As the clouds moved across the sky, members of the audience screamed, "See her! See her!"
>
> People in the audience whipped out cameras to photograph the clouds and light.
>
> "I saw baby Jesus for an instant in the sky," said Koreth Vargahese of Houston.
>
> One woman was treated by paramedics after she began screaming.

Those people saw *something,* and no doubt their conclusions about their experience were sincere. But the gatekeepers of establishment objectivity did not admit the appearance of Jesus and doves into objective reality, because the rules require that everybody (or nearly everybody) in the crowd see the *same* phenomenon, not just *some* phenomenon. Likewise for any explanation: it has to work for anybody, never mind who. "Fact" is not anybody's experience; it states the experience of no one in particular. When the police detective says, "Just the facts please, ma'am," he is asking, What would I have seen—what would *anyone* have seen, what would no one in particular have seen—at the scene of the crime?

By definition, then, if we take the empirical rule (no personal authority) seriously, revelation cannot be the basis for fact, because it is not publicly available. Similarly, attempts to claim a special kind of experience or checking for any particular person or kind of person—male or female, black or white, tall or short—are strictly illicit. After a woman was raped by a gang of teenagers in New York City, the Reverend Al Sharpton said that there was no proof that a rape had occurred, because the victim was being attended by white doctors. In other words, white checkers' findings do not count. That is illicit; if you make different rules for black and white checkers, you are not doing science. Paranormalists who claim to have verified psychic phenomena often rely upon single experiments; later, when some other investigator fails to find the claimed effect, they reply (for instance) that the necessary psychic energy was blocked by the presence of a skeptic. That also is illicit; if the way you are checking works only for people with a sympathetic attitude, or if your results are not replicable by others in a reasonably regular fashion, you are not doing science. The same applies to Christian Scientists and others who believe in faith healing but say that attempts to check it work only for the faithful. Believers in miracles argue that miraculous events can be witnessed and understood properly only by those to whom God chooses to reveal himself. That also is illicit. If the way you are seeing and explaining works only for the religious, you are breaking the rules. And Plato's regime of philosopher-rulers who have special access to truth? Prohibited, renounced, condemned.

Well, so what?

"One man's experience is nothing if it stands alone," the great American philosopher Charles Sanders Peirce wrote a century ago.

"If he sees what others cannot, we call it hallucination. It is not 'my' experience but 'our' experience that has to be thought of; and this 'us' has indefinite possibilities."[15]

Outside a small circle of cognoscenti, Peirce's lot has been a tragic and undeserved obscurity. Yet no one better understood the social implications of science's liberal ideal of objectivity.

> Unless truth be recognized as *public*—as that of which *any* person would come to be convinced if he carried his inquiry, his sincere search for immovable belief, far enough—then there will be nothing to prevent each one of us from adopting an utterly futile belief of his own which all the rest will disbelieve. Each one will set himself up as a little prophet; that is, a little "crank," a half-witted victim of his own narrowness.[16]

In that crystalline statement Peirce penetrated to the heart of the issue as no one else has. And he hints at the honest answer to the next question—the crucial political question.

It is impossible to show that either the skeptical rule or the empirical rule is "true" in any grand or final sense. There is no way I could "prove" that the pope, say, has no final say; I can only say that, in a liberal intellectual regime, papal infallibility is strictly illicit, even immoral. There is similarly no way I could "disprove" feminist empiricism, which argues that, because men's vision of reality has been distorted by their dominant position in society, "women (or feminists, whether men or women) *as a group* are more likely to produce unbiased and objective results than are men (or nonfeminists) as a group."[17] I can only say that the rules should deny respectability to anyone's claim that some particular kind of person is favored with especially undistorted insight. That being the case, the creationist or UFO-watcher or minority separatist or whoever can go off and play his own game. As he walks away he leaves his challenge behind: "Who gave you the right to set the rules? Why is your 'science game,' with its rules built by comfortable, secular, European males, the only game in town—especially if it hurts and excludes people?"

3

The Politics of Liberal Science

Liberalism's great contribution to civilization is the way it handles conflict. No other regime has enabled large and varied groups of people to set a social agenda without either stifling their members' differences or letting conflict get out of hand. Bertrand Russell once said that "order without authority" might be taken as the motto both of political liberalism and of science. If you had to pick a three-word motto to define the liberal idea, "order without authority" would be pretty good. The liberal innovation was to set up society so as to mimic the greatest liberal system of them all, the evolution of life. Like evolutionary ecologies, liberal systems are centerless and self-regulating and allow no higher appeal than that of each to each in an open-ended, competitive public process (a game). Thus, a market game is an open-ended, decentralized process for allocating resources and legitimizing possession, a democracy game is an open-ended, decentralized process for legitimizing the use of force, and a science game is an open-ended, decentralized process for legitimizing belief. Much as creatures compete for food, so entrepreneurs compete for business, candidates for votes, and hypotheses for supporters. In biological evolution, no outcome is fixed or final—nor is it in capitalism, democracy, science. There is always another trade, another election, another hypothesis. In biological evolution, no species, however clever or complex, is spared the rigors of competition—nor are the participants in capitalism, democracy, science. No matter who you are, you must conduct your business in the currency of dollars, votes, or criticism—no special fiat, no personal authority.

To think of democracy and capitalism as liberal social systems is, of course, commonplace today. To think of science that way is more challenging. Most of us think of science as a kind of machine whose equations and labs and research papers inexorably grind out data and theories and inventions. But philosophers of science have moved sharply away from that view, and toward what has become known as evolutionary epistemology. Evolutionary epistemology holds that our knowledge comes to us not from revelation, as religious traditions maintain; nor from deep reflection by the wise, as in Plato; nor even from crisp experiments that unambiguously reveal nature's secrets, as in the mechanistic view of science that prevailed until this century. Rather, our knowledge *evolves*—with all the haphazardness and improvisation that "evolving" implies. In biological evolution, species and their genes evolve as they compete for limited resources, with mutations providing the raw material for change. In evolutionary epistemology, hypotheses and ideas evolve as they compete under pressure from *criticism*, with intellectual diversity providing the raw material for change. The evolutionary view of knowledge recognizes that, in science, trial and error play as important a role as does mechanistic experimentation. It recognizes that scientific consensus doesn't always march methodically toward a single inevitable conclusion; the consensus often meanders or drifts, and where it comes out on any given day can depend as much on circumstance and fashion, even on personalities, as on nature. (Which is not to say that the results are random; the method of trial and error may be unpredictable in the short term, but in the longer term it produces steady improvement. The path may veer this way or that, but the long-term direction is uphill.) Most important, the evolutionary view recognizes that knowledge comes from a *social* process. Knowledge comes from people checking with each other. Science is not a machine; it is a society, an ecology. And human knowledge, like the species themselves, is a product of the turmoil of the interreactions of living organisms.

Order emerging as each interreacts with each under rules which are the same for all (order without authority): just as that idea links the great liberal systems, so it also links the great liberal theorists. Darwin is known to have been strongly influenced by the economic ideas of Adam Smith. "The theory of natural selection," writes Stephen Jay Gould, a paleontologist and historian of science, "is a creative transfer to biology of Adam Smith's basic argument for a rational economy: the balance and order of nature does not arise from a higher, external (divine) control, or from the existence of laws operating directly upon the whole, but from struggle among individuals for their own benefits."[1] And Adam Smith was deeply familiar with the thinking of the British political liberals (he published *The Wealth of Nations* in 1776, after all). Yet the most intimate connection between members of the liberal constellation is also the least appreciated: the connection between democracy and science. Indeed, the theory of political liberalism and the theory of epistemological liberalism were fathered by one and the same man, the father of liberalism itself.

John Locke proposed, three hundred years ago, that the legitimacy of a government resides not with the rulers but with the rolling consent of the governed. To the argument that "no government will be able long to subsist, if the People may set up a new Legislative, whenever they take offence at the old one," Locke replied that government based on popular consent will be more rather than less stable than a regime in which the ruler is fixed, initial impressions notwithstanding.[2] The genius of Locke (and, later, of Adam Smith and Charles Darwin) was to see, as Plato had not, that social stability does not require social stasis; just the opposite, in fact.

This same John Locke also set on its feet the empirical theory of knowledge. Locke himself never explicitly linked his philosophy of knowledge with his philosophy of politics, but the kinship is not hard to see. To begin with, he was one of the greatest of all the fallibilists (or, in that sense, of the skeptics). Just as no one is absolutely entitled to claim the right to rule, so no one is absolutely entitled to decide what is true. Just as not even a king may infringe on basic rights, so not even the wisest or holiest man may claim to be above error. For any and all of us may be mistaken. "All men are liable to error," Locke said. "Good men are men still liable to mistakes, and are sometimes warmly engaged in errors, which they take for divine truths, shining in their minds with the clearest light."[3] No: however certain you may feel, however strongly you are convinced, *you must check*. Knowledge of all things except our own being, God's being, and mathematics can be obtained only by looking to experience— that is, by checking. From Locke, then, comes our public process for picking worthy beliefs, as well as our public process for picking

worthy leaders. From him comes liberalism's defining principle: rule
by rules, not by persons.

And—no surprise, this—from him also comes the strongest of all
arguments for toleration of dissent. In passages which today define
the morality of liberal science, Locke preached the sermon which
every generation learns with such difficulty and forgets with such
ease: "We should do well to commiserate our mutual ignorance, and
endeavor to remove it in all the gentle and fair ways of information,
and not instantly treat others ill, as obstinate and perverse, because
they will not renounce their own, and receive our opinions. . . . For
where is the man that has incontestable evidence of the truth of all
that he holds, or of the falsehood of all he condemns?"[4] This, finally,
is why the Constitution protects the speech of Nazis, Communists,
racists, sexists, homophobes, and Andy Rooney: they may be right.
And, if they turn out to be wrong, it does us good to hear what they
have to say so that we can criticize their beliefs and know *why* they
are wrong.[5]

Wrote Madison, "As long as the reason of man continues fallible,
and he is at liberty to exercise it, different opinions will be formed."
His words echoed Locke. When the founders of the American republic
headed the Bill of Rights with "Congress shall make no law respecting
an establishment of religion, or prohibiting the free exercise thereof;
or abridging the freedom of speech, or of the press," it was Locke's
epistemology no less than his political theory which had shaped their
thinking.

By now the advantages and disadvantages of democracy and markets have been pretty thoroughly pawed over, but they deserve a
cursory glance for the light they cast on liberal science. The disadvantages are serious, and must not be passed over lightly. First, the
notion of empowering a vast, amorphous, unsupervised mass of voters
and traders to make crucial social decisions defies all common sense
and intuition. Instinct sides with Plato: it makes more sense to have
the wisest man decide who gets what or who should rule. That is
why learning democratic values and market values, which make the
judgments of democratic and market systems "feel" right, takes centuries of cultural development and years of personal education; it is

why people who are used to an authoritarian moral climate have such a hard time switching to the mechanisms of democracy and markets, and so often make a botch of it.

Second, open-ended, decentralized decision-making systems are perpetually unsettling. They cannot be counted on to reach any particular result, and often, since they put no one in particular in charge, they reach results which don't particularly please anyone. The only constant is change, and change is unnerving and sometimes painful and wasteful. Leaders go in and out of power, sometimes too quickly to hold any course; markets shut factories and move jobs. No one can count on staying on top.

But the advantages of the two systems are enormous. They are flexible, which means that they adapt readily to change. They are broadly inclusive, and so make the most of human diversity. (Anyone can vote, anyone can own.) Yet by and large they are stable, despite being both flexible and broadly inclusive. And so they are liberal in this important sense: they allow us to be relatively free to be ourselves, each to make the contribution that suits him, with comparatively little risk of upending the whole system.

The strengths and weaknesses of liberal science are much like those of its two liberal cousins. As with the other two, the disadvantages are serious.

For one, it is, if anything, harder to trust the shapeless mob of independent critical inquirers to decide what is true than it is to trust markets to allocate resources or elections to choose leaders. We all like to think of ourselves as unusually insightful, and we all have beliefs to which we cling for support and reassurance; but when we play the game of liberal science, we are at least as likely to lose as to win. If you are going to play the science game, you must take seriously Locke's demanding injunction: "The strength of our persuasions is no evidence at all of their own rectitude."[6] Never mind how sure you feel, says Locke; you have to be checked. Understandably, many strongly persuaded people say, "No, thank you." Our Platonic instinct rebels: Why allow the foolish to check the wise? Why allow the wrong to rule? Why allow moronic racists or benighted atheists to go around spreading their toxic manure? It must count as a severe practical disadvantage that a great mass of people will always look upon liberal science as senseless or immoral.

Moreover, it is not easy to love a system which never finally ends an argument. No final say; no final knowledge. That is the rule. In science, phlogiston is succeeded by oxygen, ether by vacuum; even our most basic concepts—the absoluteness of time itself, the Euclidean geometry of space, the singleness of reality, the fundamental separateness of one place from another—all are summoned before the court of critical inquiry and found unworthy. How big is the universe? This big (estimated in earth radii):

Ptolemy (A.D. 150)	20,000
Copernicus (1543)	7,850,000
Tycho Brahe (1602)	14,000
Kepler (1609)	34,177,000
Kepler (1619)	60,000,000
Galileo (1632)	2,160
Riccioli (1651)	200,000
Huygens (1698)	660,000,000
Newton (1729)	20 billion
Herschel (1785)	10,000 billion
Shapley (1920)	1,000,000 billion
Current estimate	100,000 billion

"Surveying this record is hardly likely to convince the general reader that today's solutions will fare better than their predecessors," remarks Derek Gjertsen, to whom I am indebted for the figures.[7] The same is true in economics, history, the whole restless expanse of human knowledge. The science game moves along by its own internal logic, not the logic of common sense; because its reference point is the experience of no one in particular, its picture of the world is alien to everybody. We travel from one reality to the next, like passengers on a strange tour bus, but we never arrive. The game of liberal science satisfies our craving for new beauties but not our appetite for final truth: No final say.

Ever since the skeptical revolution, many great minds have confronted this problem. Montaigne himself, unable to stand the heat of the fire he had lit, fled from the kitchen. "I accept other people's choice and stay in the position where God put me," he at last declared. "Otherwise I could not keep myself from rolling about incessantly. Thus I have, by the grace of God, kept myself intact, without agitation or disturbance of conscience, in the ancient beliefs of our religion."[8]

Who can blame him? Ralph Waldo Emerson said: "God offers to every mind its choice between truth and repose. Take which you please,—you can never have both." Personally, I find the science game's shifting otherworldly landscapes energizing and lovely. No artist has made anything nearly as vast and beautiful and challenging as our protean, dazzling, mystifying, enlightening, damnable vision of reality. But who does not also yearn for repose? Who cannot sympathize with the Christian fundamentalist who told V. S. Naipaul: "In the modern view, the world is just one damned thing after another. A *horrible* worldview. Ultimately, a worldview that human beings cannot live with. It cannot last. It will destroy itself."[9]

But here is a funny thing. Democracy has not crumbled into anarchy or ossified into a tyranny of the majority, as its enemies expected and as many of its friends feared. Capitalism has not been its own executioner, as Marx predicted it would be. And the intellectual regime built on boundless, centerless criticism has not destroyed itself or degenerated into babble. In its very strangeness, its messiness, and its amorphous vastness lies its redemption.

If you look for a liberal culture's knowledge, you will not find it set down as a list of statements in a book, nor will you find it in anyone's head. You will have to look at what people are *doing*; and you will find their picture of reality, their knowledge, flashing over the network of their daily interactions. Liberal science—science in its broadest sense—is not a system of beliefs or a constellation of authorities. Rather, it is a social community. As Peirce said, in that deep and suggestive phrase, "It is not 'my' experience but 'our' experience that has to be thought of; and this 'us' has indefinite possibilities." His "us" is the society of liberal science, the critical society: *a community of people looking for each other's mistakes.* And the "indefinite possibilities" are the fruits of human intellectual diversity when it is cultivated efficiently.

Diversity of biological form is the raw material of natural selection. Diversity of political inclination renews democratic governments and cracks authoritarian ones. Diversity of ability and of desire impels markets. And diversity of belief, thought, experience—the diversity of our various subjective worlds—is no less important. It is, indeed, among the richest of all natural resources; perhaps it is the richest of all.

If an intellectual regime is to marshal this resource effectively, it must be able to do at least two things. First, it must generate productive conflict. It must spark new ideas and open up new debates at the right places and the right times, thus setting a fruitful agenda for thought and research. Second, the system must be able to resolve the conflicts that it cultivates. After it cultivates, it must sort. It must decide *which* new ideas are worthy of research, *which* arguments are worth continuing, *which* beliefs will finally enter the canon of "general acceptance" and taken-for-granted use. The sorting is the harder half of the job. We can all have three new ideas every day before breakfast; the trouble is, they will almost always be bad ideas. The hard part is figuring out who has a *good* idea. In the absence of a peaceful way of bringing conflicting opinions into some useful juxtaposition and then choosing, our millions of ideas will just sit there, each with its own champion—no way to decide, no convergence, just schism and drift.

Of course you can rely on a central authority to set the agenda and do the sorting, but that can lead to some odd results. One of my favorite examples is an incident that occurred in 1988, when the Reverend Sun Myung Moon, the messianic leader of the Unification Church, rather dramatically added to the church's body of knowledge by announcing that his son Heung Jin Nim, who had died at the age of seventeen in a car crash, had been reincarnated in the body of a visiting church member from Zimbabwe—a conclusion which created (said the *Washington Post*) "a theological uproar among Moon's followers."[10] Authoritarian intellectual regimes confer advantage, not upon the sturdiest ideas, but upon the ones that the leadership likes. You can always count on them to waste their energy on controversies that begin with stupid ideas and lead nowhere.

My contention is that liberal science works much better as agenda-setter and idea-sorter than anything else. It has succeeded in harnessing conflict of opinion where other systems are threatened by it. It is better and faster than any other regime at moving intellectual resources—fine minds, specialized knowledge—where they can do the most good. Let me try to sketch the way the liberal-science mechanism works, because it is this mechanism into which the new enemies of inquiry are now pouring sand.

"The difference between the amoeba and Einstein," Karl Popper said, "is that, although both make use of the method of trial and error-elimination, the amoeba dislikes erring while Einstein is intrigued by it: he consciously searches for his errors in the hope of learning by their discovery and elimination."[11] Thus Popper's amoeba metaphorically "knows" some things—how to find food, how to give you dysentery—but it cannot be said to be curious. Curiosity is not merely a desire to find truth, as such; it is also a desire to find error: to find new beliefs which correct the inadequacies of old ones.

If you want to have plenty of ideas from which to choose, you have to stimulate people to be more like Einstein than the amoeba. A critical society—a community of error-seekers—stimulates curiosity by rewarding people, rather than punishing them, for finding mistakes. In the culture of liberal science, curiosity is itself a social value, entirely apart from its utility. The word "original" is high praise; unorthodoxy, if not always greeted with ecstasy, is understood to be useful; and every young scholar seeks to make a mark by extending thought in some new direction. With a successful shaking of the established view of the world comes not a prison cell but a Nobel Prize.

Think about how you get to be famous in science, journalism, history, and so on. You can develop a new hypothesis and then give it to the community to check. If it captures people's interest and starts an argument, you're famous. You are an agenda-setter. Or you can be an opinion-tester. You can become famous by entering an existing dispute, or attacking an existing problem, with a successful means of resolution. You provide a "breakthrough." At some level, of course, those two things—opening a question and resolving one— are really two sides of the same thing. Most new tests resolve old questions while creating new ones. If someone seems to do more of the former than the latter, he is regarded as especially successful. He is adjudged to have corrected error.

The chase for glory is a race to get to the next test: a race not to end the game (it never ends) but to advance it. The system is always in motion and is often very competitive: "Laboratories in the United States and Europe are in a neck-and-neck race to learn whether any new families of fundamental subnuclear particles remain to be discovered, and the finish line is now only a few months away," the *New York Times* said in an article that read just like a sports story.[12] The system's institutionalization of curiosity and its insistence on checking are the keys to its rapid adaptability. If you have an idea to defend, you have to be willing to think fast and watch out for unexpected challenges, or you'll lose the game. Constant checking requires constant readjustment, in people's heads as well as in the whole community.

That is not to say that everyone in the system will be undogmatic all the time; that is impossible, and in fact undesirable. Although the popular image of the scientist has him placidly following his experiments wherever they lead, anyone who looks at science up close quickly discovers, not surprisingly, that this is not the whole story. Physics, psychology, history—all are energized by pigheaded-ness: by people's taking positions and standing by them. Scientists often refuse to change their minds; as a last resort they sometimes insist that later developments will vindicate them, as Darwin did in the face of some really formidable genetic and geothermal objections to his theory of evolution. (Darwin hung on tenaciously when the more apparently "scientific" choice would probably have been to throw in the towel; as it turned out, later developments *did* vindicate him.) People often perform experiments and dive into research, not with wide-open minds, but because they want to vindicate their prejudices or to "get that bastard."

And, within reason, that's fine. It is important to see that the game of science allows you to feel sure you have the right answer—*as long as* you play by the rules, submitting yourself to criticism and staying in the game even when it goes against you. If you do that, you can be as dogmatic as you like, but the *system* will be undogmatic. A science writer I know once said of a famous biologist, "He's as dogmatic as they come, but he also knows the rules of the game as well as anyone." As long as that biologist sticks to the rules—claiming no final say, no personal authority—his pigheadedness serves society by making his opponents work harder, although he risks being isolated and passed by in the end. The great geologist Charles Lyell went to his grave in 1875 a holdout against the notion of human evolution, and Einstein never could accept the randomness of quantum theory ("God does not play dice"). The system adapts even if many of the individuals within it do not.

The genius of liberal science lies not in doing away with dogma and prejudice; it lies in *channeling* dogma and prejudice—making them socially productive by pitting dogma against dogma and prejudice against prejudice. Science remains unbiased even though scientists are not. "One of the strengths of science," the philosopher and historian of science David L. Hull has written, "is that it does not require that scientists be unbiased, only that different scientists have different biases."[13]

That is a crucial point. One of the creationists' and minority activists' most seductive arguments is that they should get equal time in textbooks because, after all, Darwinians and Eurocentrists are no more immune from bias than creationists and Afrocentrists. The answer is, *of course* evolutionists and Eurocentrists are biased. Biases and prejudices make us human and give sparkle to our minds. What is to be condemned is not bias but *unchecked* bias. The point of liberal science is not to be unprejudiced (which is impossible); the point is to recognize that your own bias might be wrong and to submit it to public checking by people who believe differently.

In 1988 the Anti-Defamation League of B'nai B'rith, arguing for special laws against hate-motivated crime, said, "Importantly, laws which more severely punish violent manifestations of anti-Semitism and bigotry demonstrate the country's resolve to work toward the elimination of prejudice." For private groups such as the ADL and the National Association for the Advancement of Colored People, as well as for parents and preachers, "elimination of prejudice" is indeed a worthy goal. It is worthy, too, for individuals. But different people and groups will have different ideas of what constitutes prejudice. (Is secular humanism prejudice against Christians? Is Afrocentrism prejudice against whites?) That is why eliminating prejudice is exactly what "the country"—meaning its governmental authorities—must resolve *not* to do. The same goes for universities, whose moral charter is to seek knowledge through criticism, not to instill correct opinions. For not only is wiping out bias and hate impossible in principle, in practice eliminating prejudice through central authority means eliminating all but one prejudice—that of whoever is most politically powerful.

Moreover—and this is a point far too often missed or glossed over—we all benefit enormously from living in a society which is rich with prejudices, because strong opinions, however biased or wrongheaded, energize debate. It is a positive good to have among us some racists and anti-Semites, some Christian-haters and some rabid fundamentalists. An enlightened, and efficient, intellectual regime lets a million prejudices bloom, including hateful ones. It avoids any attempt to stamp out prejudice, because stamping out prejudice inevitably means making everybody share the *same* prejudice, and thus killing science. Rather, it pits people's prejudices against each other. Then it sits back and watches knowledge evolve.

It is the pitting of opinions against each other, the insistence that anyone can err and that everyone must be checked, which gives liberal science two of its most attractive traits. First, liberal science makes a lot of mistakes. Second, however, it corrects its mistakes by rewarding those who find them.

Stephen Jay Gould writes: "Orthodoxy can be as stubborn in science as in religion. I do not know how to shake it except by vigorous imagination that inspires unconventional work and contains within itself an elevated potential for inspired error." "Inspired error": no two words could better capture the intellectual spirit of a liberal society. The notion that error is never a crime—may indeed be an inspiration—frees us to think imaginatively, even ridiculously. At the same time, the insistence that everybody be checked gives us some reassurance that the truly ridiculous will be weeded out. Herd-thinking and fad-following will always be part of human life, but over time liberal science does tend to correct itself. It shares with evolution, capitalism, and democracy this advantage of liberal systems: the capacity to be self-regulating, to be "led by an invisible hand" (order without authority). When opinion rushes to extremes, claims start being overblown, and then they become juicy targets for debunking. Pretty soon headlines appear along the lines of "Skeptics Are Challenging Dire 'Greenhouse' Views" and "Nuclear Winter Theorists Pull Back."

An old saw is that mythmaking relies on imagination where science sticks to good old hard facts. That is nonsense. "Inspired error" requires an active imagination; it requires, indeed, that the imagination be worked overtime. When the space probe Voyager flew past Neptune, one dazzled astronomer said, "Voyager has shown us we aren't using our imagination enough."[14] The difference between a scientific society and a mythmaking group is not that one relies on imagination while the other does not; it is that the skeptical and empirical rules set up a tension which makes imagination its own watchman. For if you play the game well, you must be imaginative in two ways at once: in dreaming up statements about the external world, and in dreaming up ways to debunk them.

The still more productive tension is between the fact of human intellectual diversity and the rule requiring that no one have personal authority. The importance of that rule is that it is fundamentally consensual.

Now, when I talk about consent I don't mean to say that liberal inquirers agree on much. They are a joyfully, fiercely, sometimes viciously argumentative lot. Hull writes, "The altercations that arise in science from its competitive aspects are as intrinsic to it as is the camaraderie that results from its more cooperative side."[15] So they are. But the name of the game is to make knowledge and score credit for it, and you get credit only when your conclusions are checked out by others. Others must be able to rely on your conclusions, confirm your results, trace your logic, get hold of your data. So the game of science forces you to build bridges. You must *persuade*.

Science, Peter Medawar said in a famous phrase, is the art of the soluble. I propose a refinement: science is the art of the adjudicable. When inconclusive checking breaks down into shouting, the incentives drive both sides to turn toward questions which are resolvable, or to disaggregate disputes into searches for common ground. A good example is this one, reported in the *New York Times:*

> Scientific rivals in a bitter dispute over the extinction of the dinosaurs have agreed to a hammer-wielding showdown in the mountains of central Italy next month.
>
> Rock hammers in hand, and under the watchful eye of a neutral referee, rival teams of scientists . . . will try to gather evidence both groups can accept regarding the question of why the dinosaurs died out. . . .
>
> On past expeditions by one side or the other, each gathered evidence that favored its own theory, and there was no agreement on even the most basic factual matter. If the joint expedition reaches such agreement, scientists hope, it might cool tempers that have often flared during the decade-long debate, which has involved hundreds of scientists in many countries.[16]

The game of science was doing what it does best: playing diversity of belief off against the requirement for consent, and thus channeling the energy of conflict. It was forcing people with strong opinions to find something they could agree on. The best example I know of liberal science's ability to turn a divisive dispute into a search for common ground was the birth of modern geology two hundred years ago.

In the eighteenth century, geology in its modern empirical form did not yet exist. Earth science was notorious for having produced big speculative theories which usually were not checkable, since they assumed various kinds of miraculous interventions by God (for instance, a Noachian flood). By the end of the century, theories were taking on a more empirical cast, but a decisive event was the emergence in Britain of an angry dispute. It concerned the origin of granites and basalts. Followers of one big school (Neptunians) held that granite had crystallized from a universal ocean that covered the earth in its original, chaotic state; the other school (Vulcanists) said that granite was of volcanic origin. The dispute reached a high pitch of viciousness and ill feeling. "Ridicule and irony were weapons more frequently employed than argument by the rival sects," the great geologist Charles Lyell recalled in 1835, "till at last the controversy was carried on with a degree of bitterness almost unprecedented in questions of physical science."[17] In Edinburgh a play written by a Vulcanist was booed on opening night by an audience deliberately packed with Neptunians. The conflict had gotten out of hand.

The reaction was just what you might expect: by the beginning of the nineteenth century, a skeptical backlash had formed against all geological theorizing. Speculative dreaming about the world's origin, as one geologist said in the second decade of the 1800s, was "a species of mental derangement."[18] A younger generation of earth historians declared that, instead of engaging in fruitless argument over "fanciful" theories, geology could have no proper business but to go out and find facts—specimens, for example, and fossils and geological formations. John Kidd went so far as to proclaim in 1815 that "the science of geology is at present so completely in its infancy as to render hopeless any attempt at successful generalization, and may therefore be induced to persevere with patience in the accumulation of usefull facts."[19]

And accumulate facts the geologists did—a "fact," of course, being something concrete that they could agree on. The Geological Society of London was formed in 1807 to draw upon "the labours and talents of many individuals thus united and assisted." The new conception saw geology as a decentralized science, a sum of small parts: the domain of many individuals, each contributing his share of facts, rather than of a few rival theorists and their followers. The geologists of the day were quite explicit about what was going on: they were tired of the fighting and they intended to curtail it by putting sole practitioners and uncheckable mystics out of business. The need for facts, wrote one geologist, made earth science the object "of social and united exertion, and put it quite out of the power of an individual to proceed far, without the assistance of others."[20] In other words, there would be no claims to knowledge where there could be no consent.

Miracles are, by definition, impossible to check publicly or systematically, which means that people who insist on miracles typically wind up in purely personal disputes which pit one person's word against another's. Such disputes lead to ugly incidents, even creed wars. Not surprisingly, it was largely during the early nineteenth century that miracles were abolished and checking was made the sine qua non of competent geology. (That's the empirical rule: Show me.) Geologists systematized their debate by eliminating all reference to supernatural caprice in explaining natural events. It was also during this period that geological theorists respectfully but irrevocably cut themselves loose from the biblical account of the earth's history, as the belief in a worldwide Noachian flood grew harder to square with the growing accretion of facts. By 1823 a geologist could say what had been unthinkable a few decades before: "for the sake of revelation as well as of science—of truth in every form—the physical part of the inquiry ought to be conducted as if the Scriptures were not in existence."[21] (That's the skeptical rule: No pre-set conclusion.) With the two liberal rules in place, modern geology, with its associations and publications and international network of explorers and checkers, rapidly took shape. By 1830 or so the Neptunian-Vulcanist schism had been resolved and made obsolete (the accumulating evidence had vindicated the Vulcanists), and earth historians had reconstituted their discipline as an open-ended, decentralized liberal science.

The constant threat to any social system for choosing between ideas is schism. That was the threat which the geologists of two hundred years ago were confronted with. Their success in coping with it illustrates an important point. One of liberal science's greatest triumphs is what it has *not* done: split apart. We do not have two or ten incompatible kinds of physics or history, each denying the legitimacy of the others; there has been no Great Schism in science. "Scientific investigation has had the most wonderful triumphs in the

way of settling opinion," Peirce wrote in 1877, making a point which
has been too little noticed since. Liberal science has two invaluable
social skills. First, it is very good at resolving conflicts. Second, it is
very good at *not* resolving conflicts. A critical society is capacious.
Because no one claims the final say, people leave each other room
to disagree, and then to agree to disagree—which is surely one of
science's most important tools. The process can flow around disagreements, when they prove intractable, by defining them away or by
coming back to them later with new tests in hand, or simply by
leaving them to one side. Liberal science is saved from schism by its
ability to encompass contradictory views, allowing them to compete
and coexist until one or all are at last eliminated or outmoded. That
is the hidden power in these four capacious words: We don't yet
know.

Indeed, the best way to think of liberal science is not as a consensus
of opinion or a body of knowledge, but as a self-organizing swirl of
disagreements. Many of the arguments are intense, but hardly ever
do they involve enough people to upset more than a small part of
the whole system. Liberal science's best protection is its sprawling,
encompassing vastness; it spans continents and generations. This is
also the key to its efficiency. When you make hypotheses public and
allow anyone (in principle) to try to debunk them, you can quickly
put an idea together with whoever in the world is best able to check
it. Through journals, associations, newspapers, conferences, a proposition stated in Berlin can be almost immediately tested and modified
by strangers in Buenos Aires, Beijing, or Birmingham; it can be
checked fifty years from now by people unborn today. As the critical
society reaches out for new disputes and new ways to solve them,
the network of checkers rapidly grows and deepens. Derek J. de Solla
Price found that the number of scientists and journals has tended to
double every ten to fifteen years since Locke's day; "using any reasonable definition of a scientist, we can say that 80 to 90 per cent of all
the scientists that have ever lived are alive now."[22] Since World War
II between one hundred and four hundred new scientific journals
have been introduced *every year*. In the critical society, national
boundaries have long since disappeared. Between 1975 and 1984

alone, in the leading industrial nations, internationally coauthored research publications roughly doubled as a percentage of the total, and the rate of growth was accelerating.[23] Newton said he stood on the shoulders of giants. Yes, but more important still is that liberal science allows each of us to stand on the shoulders of millions of ordinary inquirers, not just the few great ones. Authoritarian systems have their intellectual giants. What they lack is the capacity to organize and exploit their masses of middling thinkers. As the geologists of the early nineteenth century seemed to realize, great science is often the sum of small contributions. In 1989 an astronomer finally identified an obscure object 84 trillion miles away; his children had grown up in the time it took him to show that the object of his long-time study was a pair of so-called brown dwarfs. Multiply his effort thousands and millions of times, and a picture of the universe gradually emerges.

Peter Medawar has said, "Science, broadly considered, is incomparably the most successful enterprise human beings have ever engaged upon."[24] Coming from a professional biologist, that statement is somewhat self-serving; yet on the whole it is probably fair. What accounts for science's success? Intelligence, creativity, and perseverance on the part of its practitioners, certainly. But intelligence, creativity, and perseverance are not unique to scientists or liberals—far from it. The answer is above all to be found in the science game's power as a social organizer. Liberal science is successful as a problem-solver above all because of its prowess as a problem-*finder* and a problem-*attacker*. It puts millions of people to work on millions of problems, letting each go where his interests and talents lead and where the rewards are greatest. It deploys more minds and allows them greater play than can any externally directed system. In other words, it uses resources well.

Add together the millions of people proposing and checking ideas, and you get a process which is messy, uncontrolled, and often baffling; yet it is also, somehow, orderly, responsive, and able to deploy formidable intellectual resources with sometimes breathtaking speed. Just think of the attack on AIDS, a case study in the way disorganized organization can use the promise of prestige and fame and (of course) money to exploit an intellectual community of immense variety and depth. Or think about the cold-fusion episode. In March 1989 two chemists created a sensation by announcing that they had achieved nuclear fusion at room temperature. A month later the *New York Times* reported that scientists were "operating an informal, round-the-clock, worldwide symposium on cold fusion by means of facsimile machines and electronic bulletin boards."[25] And before four months had elapsed, the community of checkers had produced its first provisional verdict: false. I don't mean to direct attention only to the hard sciences. The "softer" fields—economics, political theory, sociology, history, even journalism—rarely produce unambiguous results, but they are hardly less global or responsive.

As we check and criticize and find common ground, as we propose ideas and they fall apart and we try again, our knowledge advances. The picture of the world so produced is not a neat set of consistent statements, all lined up in rows under the proper headings; it is a seething ecology of hypotheses in constant flux and competition and contradiction. The core of our present knowledge (the earth revolves around the sun) is pretty well settled, but the edges are an exploratory riot. And the whole clamorous affair reinvents itself as it goes along.

Of course, liberal science misses a lot of bets. It achieves sorry failures. It lets many people work on problems which may not be among the most pressing. On the whole, though, whenever you set everyone loose to check anyone through public criticism and competition for consent, you lay the groundwork for a social system whose ability to energize and organize human creativity has never been surpassed.

So far I have dwelt on the science side, as it were, of liberal science. But the liberal side is no less important. The science rules are as special for their political and moral implications as for their efficiency.

No Final Say and No Personal Authority are not just operational procedures for professional intellectuals. Socially speaking, they are also moral commandments, ethical ideals. They are a liberal society's epistemological constitution. By imposing upon us the obligation to check our opinions and to cultivate rather than curtail criticism, the science rules deprive intellectual authoritarians of all moral force. Plato's philosopher-ruler would have said that the central authorities were immoral, as well as inept, if they failed to control what ordinary people might say and believe; the science rules turn Plato's morality on its head. If you believe in the liberal ethic of criticism and checking, then you will also believe that all attempts to exert political control over knowledge and belief are wicked. And that is important in a world where Plato's morality still has its full share of supporters.

All of this came home to me in the summer of 1988, six months before Khomeini ordered Rushdie's death, when Universal Pictures' release of *The Last Temptation of Christ* elicited a wave of fury from religious fundamentalists around the United States. The movie depicted Jesus in a number of ways that departed from the mainstream Christian view. He was shown as reluctant to accept the burden of being God's appointed messiah, and as being tempted by a fantasy in which he had sex with a woman, fathered children, and led the life of an ordinary man. On August 11 twenty-five thousand people marched, sang, and chanted in protest at Universal in Los Angeles, carrying signs saying "Read the Bible," "Jesus Never Sinned," "God Will Not Be Mocked," and the like. Some Christians demanded that the film be suppressed; not long afterwards in Salt Lake City, taking matters into their own hands, burglars broke into a movie theater, stole the film, and slashed the screen. The expressions of rage and the calls for suppression went on despite the fact that virtually none of the Christian protesters had seen the movie, as they freely admitted. They were protesting what they had heard about the movie before its release and what they had seen in a draft of the screenplay (which was changed for the final version). Above all, they were protesting the very existence of an account of Jesus's life which was at odds with the account they revered. To them such a movie was an insult to the objective truth about Jesus. They would very gladly have destroyed it.

I have always found this sort of behavior fascinating as well as repugnant. At the time of the protests against *The Last Temptation*, it occurred to me that no case has yet reached my attention of crowds of enraged astronomers demanding the suppression of unorthodox astronomical theories. Nor has much blood been shed by rival tribes of economists torturing and killing each other in disputes over markets' efficiency. And I have not yet heard of any efforts on the part of scientists in particular or liberals in general to purge libraries and history books of unusual or discredited theories, or to lead inquisitions of dissenters.

We take the absence of purges and inquisitions among those who play the science game so much for granted that we forget how extraordinary the absence really is. "Until the end of the eighteenth century," the historian Arthur M. Schlesinger, Jr., notes, "torture was normal investigative procedure in the Catholic church as well as in most European states."[26] You could map a lot of human history simply by tracing the long line of creed wars within and between cultures. Creed wars are still going on today within and between orthodox groups of all kinds. But such wars have almost disappeared from critical society. Liberal science has brought peace.

The cheap explanation has always been that the use of force to settle disputes about the external world abated because reason replaced faith. No one, however, has managed to say just what reason is, and where it differs from faith. (Why is it "reason" for a layman to believe Darwin's story about human development but "faith" to believe the Bible's story?) The truth is that liberal science rests upon faith in its rules; it is not a system for doing without faith but a system for *managing* it. Many scientists understand that. "To speak of science and its continued progress," wrote Michael Polanyi, a chemist and philosopher of science, "is to profess faith in its fundamental principles and in the integrity of scientists in applying and amending these principles."[27]

Religious activists often complain that the liberal scientific order ("secular humanism") is itself a form of faith, a belief system, and so deserves no special standing. They are half right. Belief in liberal science is a faith, but it *does* deserve special standing: not only because it is the best social regime for mobilizing resources to produce knowledge, but also because it is inherently anti-authoritarian. If you care about freedom of thought, that's important. The Inquisition died, not because people dispensed with faith, but because they learned to put their faith in liberal social institutions. They committed themselves to the rules which say that no one is immune from checking and no one is in charge. Thus they established the overarching political fact of a liberal intellectual community: the power to settle differences of opinion lies with no one in particular. And no one in particular is the very safest person to entrust with that great power.

By their nature, then, the science rules smash the political legitimacy of intellectual authoritarianism. "Truth has been specially entrusted to the apostles and their successors," Pope John Paul II declared in 1989.[28] In a liberal culture, that kind of claim—a power grab, really— is illicit and repugnant. Anyone who claims to be in charge of the knowledge industry (such-and-such is true because I say so) thereby disqualifies himself from participating in it. The same goes for anyone who claims to have the last word. In a liberal society, the only legitimate way to decide who is right is through open-ended public checking of each by each, through criticism and questioning—just as in a democratic society the only legitimate arbiter of political power is the open-ended popular vote. Other claims are bogus. Anyone— pope, propagandist, anti-Communist, anti-racist—who wants to silence criticism or regulate an argument in order to keep wrong-thinking people out of power has no moral claim to be anything but ignored.

"When complete agreement could not otherwise be reached," Peirce wrote, "a general massacre of all who have not thought in a certain way has proved a very effective means of settling opinion in a country."[29] One way to settle disputes about the nature of reality is to look for a common test and, if none is found, agree to disagree and keep looking. That's liberal science. Another is to insist that you are right and begin looking for ways to eliminate those who are wrong. Probably most of us have at some point been tempted to eliminate someone whose opinion we disliked. Liberal ideals mute that impulse. In a culture in which people take seriously the possibility that the other guy might be right, killing him or shutting him up cannot *even in principle* advance the cause of knowledge. Just the opposite: it may mean missing the chance to correct a mistake. In liberal society, the impulse to stamp out wrong opinion—Plato's impulse—is nothing less than the impulse to destroy knowledge itself.

I spoke in the last chapter of the skeptical moral commandment to take seriously the idea that you might be wrong. If you look politically at someone who lives by that commandment, you find you can describe him this way: he is one who feels that it is never a crime to be mistaken. That is the central tenet of a liberal scientific morality. Locke, who so passionately pleaded the cause of the mistaken, would smile to see his morality so well established today.

So, perhaps, would another, the patron saint of the curious and the mistaken. Of the twelve disciples, one alone was not present when Jesus returned to their midst after the Crucifixion. "The other disciples therefore said unto him, 'We have seen the Lord.' But he said unto them, 'Except I shall see in his hands the print of the nails, and put my finger into the print of the nails, and thrust my hand into his side, I will not believe.' " Thus spake Thomas, the plucky empiricist. Jesus reproached him. "Thomas, because thou hast seen me, thou hast believed: blessed are they that have not seen, and yet have believed." Jesus was wise in many things, but in this matter liberal science has roundly repudiated him. The followers of Thomas say, finally: knowledge cannot be had except where criticism is unfettered and doubt is never rebuked. That is the modern liberal's skeptical faith.

Skeptical faith is not wholly satisfying. Many of Thomas's disciples remain, even today, reluctant and vaguely uneasy. Jesus, with his requirement that we put our faith in the authority of a greater mind, commands zeal and adoration; Thomas, with his faith in the common search for error, is often received tepidly even among his allies. If I have given the impression that liberal science is perfect or complete, now is the time to note, again, that it is neither. People hanker for more than it provides; they complain, understandably, about its inability to do all that a perfect intellectual regime should do.

I think that three kinds of complaint are fundamental enough to be especially worth noting.

The complaint from *spirituality* accuses liberal science of ruthlessly driving out of public intellectual life ideas and beliefs which do not conform to the science game's empirical tenets, but which human beings nonetheless need in order to live well.

The complaint from *virtue* accuses liberal science of weakening people's moral backbone by substituting a regime of anything-goes criticism for one based on venerable virtues which critics should not be encouraged to attack.

The complaint from *community* accuses liberal science of undermining social standards by permitting, even fomenting, irresponsible talk and belief, and so weakening the very community on which liberal science depends.

At bottom the complaints speak less to liberal science's badness than to its incompleteness. Let me explain with a few words about each.

The complaint from spirituality is in many respects the strongest and the most deeply felt. It says to liberal science: "Look at the vast continents of human spiritual and supernatural belief and experience, the deeps of myth and the peaks of religious revelation. All of that you relegate to the fringe of nuttiness or the interior limbo of purely mental phenomena. Are you simply going to ignore so much that is so important? Are you going to dismiss or define away what is, for millions of people, the richest part of human life? Can you so impoverish human souls, leaving them nothing but the parched findings of your sciences? If so, it is a disgrace."

Some of us—I am one—are so constituted as not to mind very much if the supernatural and the subjective are banished from our public knowledge base. But many people mind it horribly. They need to believe in a creator, a purpose, a spirit. Of course, they can believe, if they like; and most people do. One of the signal advantages of liberal science is that it does not force anyone to renounce, for instance, his belief in a divine being or his experience of an encounter with a UFO or a supernatural force. The reason liberal science can afford its hands-off policy is that it limits its domain to *public* knowledge: a body of propositions which are argued about and developed as a group effort, and which are collectively given special *social* (as opposed to personal) respectability and accorded unique standing in making public decisions (such as whether Christian Science treatment counts as medical care for legal purposes).

However, in the public realm liberal science is sovereign and nearly absolute. It sets the agenda and controls respectability. If you believe you saw an alien spacecraft, you are free to say so and think so, but in the realm of public knowledge your belief will be seen as at best an unresolved personal anomaly and at worst the imaginings of a disturbed mind. If your experience was wholly private or does not withstand public checking, it will not shape the research agenda (outside of psychology and sociology departments) and few intellectual resources will be devoted to exploring it. It will be marginalized as a curiosity.

Recall the case of Hilda, the woman who saw Elvis in her office. To the extent her experience is purely private, it is not checkable and so is off the agenda; to the extent it is checkable, it checks out false and deserves little further attention. While she is left to conclude what she likes about what happened to her, the intellectual establishment does not bother to conclude anything. It gives her not so much as a serious look or a wave hello. Her experience attracts little argument and has virtually no effect on the research agenda (except, again, for psychologists and others who want to know about her mind; no one goes to her office with instruments and cameras to look for Elvis, though some people may go in to look at her). Her experience is, in short, marginalized. And under the science rules that is the fate of purely personal experience and uncheckable belief.

For many people, the result is a kind of uneasy bifurcation of life. I have a friend, a lawyer, who in his working and public life knows all the intellectual rules and lives by them. Yet privately, among his closest friends, he talks about the spirit of God that walks among us, and about the deep truths of Indian myth. He reconciles the conflicting claims on his loyalty by keeping the two worlds apart: the subjective and personal to one side, the objective and public to the other. And that, says the science game, is just what he should do. The reality produced by the science game is nothing more or less than a set of publicly tested propositions. It is never wholly congruent with the *felt* reality of my or your or anyone's experienced world, each of which is singular and sovereign for the person who experiences it. Marginalization takes a toll. If you believe in a divine being or extrasensory perception or Elvis, then you look for public confirmation. You may join a church or group which can give it to you. But that may not be enough. You may desire the kind of high-prestige confirmation which only the science game, in a liberal society, can provide. And that kind of confirmation you cannot have. Moreover, the science game seems to extend its reach every day: so much so, that to elbow it aside you may feel you need to do what Khomeini or the Saudis or the Reverend Jim Jones did and shut out the world.

Contrary to what many have said, liberal science does not obliterate the world of the soul and the spirit. It does, however, delimit it and then leave it alone. It does so because it must. The alternative is to put nonadjudicable private beliefs at the top of the public agenda, thus destroying the peace and wasting intellectual capital on fruitless arguments (*"Which* God is real?"). From the point of view of managing a society and building knowledge, intellectual liberalism uses the best strategy available. However, a critical intellectual system cannot fill our spiritual needs and does not pretend to; it sends us off to fill them privately as best we can. It is incomplete—utterly so—as to providing for our souls.

The complaint from virtue is a little different and, to my mind, the least important. "Liberal science," it says, "is a set of rules governing *how* we strive to believe. But it does not, and cannot, tell us *what* to believe. Its seeming willingness to entertain any idea—though not to *accept* any idea—seems to say, 'You don't know for sure what's right, I don't know what's right—the system of critical exchange will decide for us, except *it* will never really know, either.' Yet humans need healthy values and strong moral fiber if they hope to live with themselves and each other. Liberal science criticizes and questions every moral precept in sight. The result is relativism and moral rot."

That is a familiar complaint against all liberal social systems, not just the intellectual one: capitalism is alleged to know the price of everything but the value of nothing, democracy to turn libertine and dithering. The contemporary philosopher Alasdair MacIntyre charges liberalism with seeing society "as nothing more than an arena in which individuals seek to secure what is useful or agreeable to them." He says, "Modern society is indeed often, at least in surface appearance, nothing but a collection of strangers, each pursuing his or her own interests under minimal constraints."[30] With the very concept of virtue lost in the pandemonium of liberalism's ethical bazaar, no wonder that "we have all too many disparate and rival moral concepts"—more than liberal culture has the moral resources to settle. "It follows that our society cannot hope to achieve moral consensus."[31] Thus has liberalism produced a kind of modern Babel; it has indeed spawned "the new dark ages which are already upon us."[32]

Does liberal science—or liberal capitalism, or liberal democracy—hasten moral rot? I doubt it: so far as I can see, a society with the illiberal political system of Brezhnev's Soviet Union, the illiberal economic system of Indira Gandhi's India, or the illiberal intellectual system of Khomeini's Iran is no likelier to be "virtuous" or decently principled than America or Western Europe. You can make a strong case that, although people in the modern liberal countries may often disagree about virtue, the countries themselves tend to behave more virtuously than any countries in history. In any case, moral disagreement is a problem in all societies, liberal or no; the question is whether you harness it or violently repress it.

It is true that the science rules cannot resolve moral questions in the way they can often lead to quick resolutions of questions of fact. You can't perform a study or run an experiment to determine whether abortion is murder or capital punishment is cruel. However, let it be said in favor of the science rules that they can help bring order and peacefulness to moral debate. Insisting on criticism and checking can at least help keep moral arguments from degenerating into shouting matches or worse. And it *can*, albeit over time and haphazardly, tease out an enlightened consensus. Year after year, critics demanded a reason natural rights or equality should extend only to men who looked like "us"; one reason after another was shot down, and eventually the moral legitimacy of slavery and racism collapsed. Liberal science's regime of criticism did not "prove" slavery wrong but clearly did help to kill it.

There is, however, this bit of justice in the complaint from virtue: No Final Say and No Personal Authority are not an all-encompassing morality or a rounded code of ethics for human life. We still need compassion, honesty, decency, loyalty, respect for the future, and so on. All societies need those things. The existence of a critical culture does not demonstrably undermine them, but it also does nothing to guarantee them. And so, although liberal science can help people organize the search for decent moral principles, it is incomplete as to providing them.

I save for last the complaint from community, because right now it is the most pressing and challenging of the three. It sounds somewhat like the complaint from virtue but takes a more pragmatic turn. "For liberal science to exist," goes the argument, "it has to have a community: a polity, a university, or what have you. Yet it allows, sometimes even encourages, the sorts of irresponsible and foolish talk and belief which erode the community's strength. By standing for nothing except universal doubt and criticism, it undermines the standards on which it depends. To defend itself *and* to defend liberal inquiry, the community has the right, indeed the responsibility, to draw the line at certain kinds of irresponsible talk or belief and say, 'This we will not tolerate.' "

Here is an appealing argument which, up to a point, has an element of sense in it; but it hides razor blades, too. People who complain of nettlesome criticism on the grounds that it undermines "community standards" are usually smuggling in a treacherous assumption: that they know what the community thinks, and that it is more or less the same as what *they* think. Such people are, necessarily, either majoritarians who object to a minority opinion or elitists who object to a majority opinion. Either way, it is unclear why they have any special standing to regulate discussion in the name of the whole community.

For, of course, communities don't have opinions or speak their minds. People do. Liberal science's great discovery was that within *every* community is a wide variety of opinion, enough to fuel the arguments that propel knowledge forward. In liberal science, the community discovers what it thinks through criticism—and its members never do all think any one thing. If they did, intellectual progress would stop.

What about the foolish crank or the irresponsible hatemonger? By giving those people free rein, doesn't liberal science tacitly encourage verbal outrages and irresponsible sloganeering? Not really. Quietly but inexorably working in the science game is the disciplinary mechanism of marginalization. Though the rules of the game do not allow majorities to repress other people's opinions, they do give them every right to shrug them off. People who are irresponsible, who bruit about opinions but won't stand to be checked or won't abide by the results, are dismissed as nutty or obnoxious. People who go around saying that the Holocaust didn't happen are pushed to the fringes. Liberal science tends to discourage such people by marginalizing them.

So, I think, on the communitarians' own premises, the *mechanism* of liberal science is a good social system to choose if you care about peacefully holding together a diverse community while systematically keeping irresponsible voices on the fringes, where they belong.

But does the *ethic* of liberal science undermine its own community? Defenders of community standards are right to say that science needs community to exist. But they are wrong if they think it needs a community of people with like opinions. The community of liberal science is defined by agreement on *rules:* by a mutual undertaking to check and be checked.

On paper, there may be reason to worry that the critical community might undermine its own strength by tolerating nonsense or criticizing itself to death. However, after several hundred years of nonsense and criticism from one quarter after another, the community of liberal science has outlived all its challengers. It has, in effect, criticized itself and emerged the stronger. It has outlived, too, millions of cranks and venom-spewers. The center is holding: in fact, the liberal community of checkers is growing, not shrinking. So is the community of democracy; so is the community of capitalism. Thus the argument that liberalism militates against its own community shows every sign of being wrong.

And yet, and yet. There is something in the communitarian argument which continues to nag. What? I think a professor I know put his finger on it when he told me in a letter:

> In my debates with the fundamentalist left, the main driving force seems to be a sense of impotence. So much that is so bad is going on, and they can do nothing. At least professors have some power in their universities. As futile as such gestures may be, we can pass rules trying to force students and our fellow professors to be nice. However, I did not sense closed minds, especially among my students. They are aware of how problematic their position is. "But if we can't do this, what can we do?" A good question.

Yes. If a society renounces the option of exiling or jailing or otherwise punishing people who say foolish or mean or irresponsible things, then it gives up its strongest social tool for showing disapproval. Yet the rules of the science game ask it to do just that. In particular, the morality of liberal science charges two kinds of institutions with an especial obligation not to punish people for what they say or believe: governments, because their monopoly on force gives them enormous repressive powers, and universities, because their moral charter is first and foremost to advance human knowledge by practicing and teaching criticism. If governments stifle criticism, then they impoverish and oppress their citizenry; if universities do so, then they have no reason to exist.

Yet on campuses and street corners verbal outrages *will* happen, because foolish and vicious people will always be with us. Generally those people will be unable to set the agenda; generally they will be kept on the fringes; generally they will (or should) be ignored. But they are ingenious and will always find ways to make mischief unless they are eliminated completely.

And so here is the third kind of incompleteness. Because liberal science undeniably does allow people to talk and believe irresponsibly, it is incomplete as to ensuring that verbal outrages won't occur.

Today, this is the kind of incompleteness that rankles the most. The Ku Klux Klansman cries, "The nigger should be returned to Africa, the Jew returned to Israel"; the rap singer declares, "If black people kill black people every day, why not have a week and kill white people?" Is it enough just to shrug and ignore those people? Is it enough to criticize? To ridicule? How about *punishing* them, positively and forcefully? Is that always such a bad idea?

To see why the answer is yes, one has to look at the enemies of the game of science and at the real-world alternatives they propose. In the remainder of this essay, we turn to confront them.

4

The Fundamentalist Threat

Fundamentalism first came into focus for me while I was working as an economic journalist in Washington. Going from one interview to the next, I began to realize that a lot of people lived in a world which looked markedly different from mine, and that the differences lay not so much in what they believed as in *how*. Those people exhibited the sort of thinking which is sometimes called dogmatic, ideological, or true believing. I wound up preferring "fundamentalism" as better capturing the flavor of the attitude I was encountering. People usually use the term in a specifically religious context, of course, but I came to think that a broader application makes more sense. Christianity and Judaism and Islam are just several of many creeds, religious and nonreligious, which one can be fundamentalist about. Just as only some religious people are fundamentalist, only some fundamentalists are religious.

Fundamentalism—the intellectual style, not the religious movement—is the strong disinclination to take seriously the notion that you might be wrong. For instance, the Ayatollah Khomeini, probably the most influential and implacable fundamentalist of our age, told an interviewer in 1979, "I do know that, during my long lifetime, I have always been right about what I said."[1] That was an amazing assertion: the man was saying that he enjoyed perfect access to truth. Now, in a predominantly scientific culture like America's, that kind of bald statement isn't common, at least not among the intellectual classes; but you do not have to look very hard to find people whose attitudes run quite a long way in the same direction.

In Washington I can show you anti-drug fundamentalism and animal-rights fundamentalism and environmental fundamentalism and feminist fundamentalism and plenty more. I can draw your attention to the creepy certitude of Marine Lt. Col. Oliver North, a

man who seemed completely unacquainted with the possibility that
he might be wrong. ("Sometimes you just have to go above the written
law," Fawn Hall, North's secretary, said about the Iran-Contra affair
of 1986. They were servants of Truth.) When I read about Ronald
Reagan's fabled incuriosity I thought, Here is a man who is not much
inclined to look for his mistakes. (After the Iran-Contra scandal broke,
Mr. Reagan's aides implored him for weeks to say he had blundered,
but the best he could finally muster was "Mistakes were made.")

As a journalist, I came to know people whom you might call
economic fundamentalists. Many of them were anti-market people
who attributed all evil to the lack of enlightened government interven-
tion in wanton markets. Do banks and savings-and-loans fail? Then
the problem is marketplace failure and the answer is tighter regulation.
Is health care too expensive and too hard for poor and jobless people
to get? Then the problem is marketplace failure and the answer is
tighter regulation. Poverty? Homelessness? Inequality? Slow growth
in incomes? Same problem, same answer. In the 1970s consumerist
fundamentalists became common: people who thought that, by definition, big business was always collusive and plunderous, incapable
of doing good without constant government supervision. Outside
America, the great focus of hard-core economic fundamentalism has
been Marxism and its offshoots. By definition, capitalism cannot work,
it cannot be other than exploitive; workers who claim not to be
exploited are ignorant or deluded, and people who say that capitalism
works are missing the deeper reality and the internal contradictions.
In Washington, however, the economic fundamentalists whom I knew
best were people in the ranks of free-marketers. I suppose they were
especially interesting because I thought that a good deal of what they
believed was true. That was challenging. It is one thing to meet an
Islamic nationalist fundamentalist, whose beliefs (that all war or poverty among Arabs is the West's fault, for instance) seem so alien and
nutty. It is quite another thing to meet someone whose beliefs are
similar to yours but are *held differently*. What to make of that? Imagine
discovering a group of Darwinist cultists, whose holy creed is evolution and whose sacred text is *The Origin of Species*. You could dismiss
their practice as not being science, but you could not dismiss their

belief as being wrong. So it was with the hard-core free-market activists. I couldn't dismiss them as economic "creationists." I also knew
them well enough to know they were not a whit less smart or well
informed or well-intentioned than I. Yet I never stopped feeling that
there was a gulf between their attitude toward truth and mine, and
I always marveled at the starkness and obviousness with which reality
had laid itself bare to them.

One man, S., was perfectly certain that a return to the gold standard
would reduce interest rates to 1 or 2 percent forever, ushering in a
new dawn of global prosperity. It could not *not* happen. Another
man, C., was just as certain that anything the government did, except
perhaps provide for defense and law enforcement, made the country
poorer for the government's having done it. That is so clear, he said,
that the politicians who create and support federal programs must
all be either evil or stupid—and he supposed they were generally
evil, because it would be hard to be so stupid. C. was no raving nut;
he was a charming, brilliant man who could be found at some of the
best parties and who got quoted in newspapers. One day, trying to
fathom the depths of his certitude, I took him through one of the
standard skeptical catechisms. Is it possible that someone as smart and
knowledgeable as you might draw the wrong conclusion sometimes,
maybe even often? Yes. Is it possible that *you* might draw the wrong
conclusion? Yes. Might you then be wrong in this case? No. Others
may be wrong, he himself may have been wrong in the past, but this
time he cannot be wrong.

Another man, P., told me that *serious* economists know that the
minimum wage throws poor people out of work and cuts off the
bottom rung of the ladder. I mentioned that quite a lot of people,
including a lot of supposedly serious economists, had concluded that
the minimum wage helps poor people, on balance. "I don't think
they believe it," P. replied. "It's too self-evident." In other words, they
are either lying or (his term) "willfully naive." I asked about their
empirical work. He replied that if a study shows that red is really
black, it is not a credible study, or it has overlooked something. "It's
like if you drop a rock it always falls, and if it doesn't, some exogenous
factor has intervened." I asked if he couldn't be mistaken, if he hadn't

been wrong in the past when he had thought he was right. He replied that, on the important questions about how the world works, he could not remember ever having been wrong as an adult. But the leftists had been wrong about everything, he said—wrong so often that they almost had to be doing it on purpose. To be so consistently wrong, they almost had to be malicious.

N., another free-marketer, was a little less rigid. "I don't get shaken much," he told me, "but I do like to get shaken every once in a while." He talked about someone he had worked with, who believed that, because government regulation can do only harm, the civil-rights laws must have harmed blacks. "The only reason he goes to the evidence is because someone else is asking for it." This style, N. said, has the advantage of letting you arrive at your conclusions quickly. "You can be paralyzed by knowledge," he said. "If you know too much on a subject, it's very gray." I asked him about his pro-government opponents: were they evil, stupid, or merely mistaken? He declined the broad brush, but thought a moment and said, "I can convince almost anyone who is not fundamentally evil or fundamentally stupid to agree with me."

Those are good people, smart people, sometimes right people. Often they pointed out what I had not seen or noticed. By advancing new or radical ideas, they made a useful contribution. They were eye-openers, consensus-pushers, complacency-breakers. Eventually they forced me to two realizations. First, you're not wrong just because you're a fundamentalist. Second, to some extent we are all fundamentalists, each and every one of us. We are all true believers in something. What distinguishes the ethic of liberal science is not that liberals are undogmatic; it is that liberals believe they must check their beliefs, or submit them for checking, *however* sure they feel. And that ethic, I finally concluded, was what made me feel so removed from the free-marketers—or the environmentalists or animal-rights activists or feminists or whomever. What distinguishes them is not the right-ness or wrongness of their beliefs, or even that they believe strongly. It is that they show no interest in checking.

In what follows, I want to analyze the fundamentalist intellectual style more deeply—its mentality, its morality, its political implications. But I do not condemn that style, simply because it would be absurd and hypocritical to do so. Seeking certainty may be as deeply embedded a human imperative as seeking food. All of us are dogmatic somewhere and sometime, and none has the right to cast the first stone. What I do condemn is the fundamentalist *social rule:* Those who know the truth should decide whose opinion is right. That rule is what is to be feared and fought. A society run on liberal intellectual rules benefits from its dogmatists and true believers by making them argue with each other. But a society run on fundamentalist intellectual rules does not benefit from free-ranging critics and cannot abide them. You can put fundamentalist raisins in the liberal cake, but you cannot very easily put the cake inside the raisins. When fundamentalism becomes institutionalized and empowers a central authority over truth, as it tends to do, it has the nasty habit of terrorizing dissenters.

My friends the free-market fundamentalists were, fortunately, people who respected nonviolence and democratic freedoms. But not all fundamentalists do. And even among pluralists the dynamics of orthodoxy are not friendly to criticism. In the 1980s the Republican party in Washington became a fundamentalist anti-tax church, whose members rallied around credos like "Raising taxes of any kind slows economic growth in both the long run and the short run," "Raising taxes can never help reduce a budget deficit, since Congress will spend every dime and then some," and so on. For the most part, the believers neither doubted nor checked their beliefs, and people in the group who did not agree with the orthodoxy held their tongues. One prominent Republican economist, who regarded the anti-tax gospel as dogma and had broken with it publicly, told me that his fellow conservatives treated him as though he had some kind of disease.

The epistemological theorists, cobweb-beclothed though they may seem, have some light to shed on modern-day movie-stompers, political zealots, and true believers. Locke's own portrait of fundamentalism—he called it "enthusiasm"—remains as vivid as ever. "They see the light infused into their understandings, and cannot be mistaken; it is clear and visible there, like the light of bright sunshine; shows itself, and needs no other proof but its own evidence: they feel the hand of God moving them within, and the impulses of the Spirit, and cannot be mistaken in what they feel." At the time, Locke was talking about religious zealots. "Whatsoever odd action they find in themselves a strong inclination to do, that impulse is concluded to be a call or direction from heaven, and must be obeyed: it is a commission from above, and they cannot err in executing it."[2] Reading Locke, one thinks of Robert L. Hymers, a Baptist minister who told the *Los Angeles Times* during the protests against *The Last Temptation of Christ*, "I think this movie is filthy! I think it is ugly! And I think it is going to bring God's fiery judgment upon America."

It was Peirce, in his magnificent essay "The Fixation of Belief" (1877), who showed how what I call the fundamentalist intellectual style is quite separate from religion. His phrase "fixation of belief" went to the heart of what fundamentalism is about. The fundamentalist temperament tends to search for certainty rather than for errors. The fundamentalist's tendency is to nail his beliefs in place.

And of course we all cling to fixed beliefs, to one degree or another. Fixation of belief is indispensable for thinking. We have to have constants (All brothers are male) if the variables are to have meaning (Some brothers are fat). The philosopher Ludwig Wittgenstein, with his incomparable gift for metaphor, said it was as though some propositions "were hardened and functioned as channels for such empirical propositions as were not hardened but fluid; and . . . this relation altered with time, in that fluid propositions hardened, and hard ones became fluid." The hardened channels' role "is like that of rules of a game"—the reality-making game. If someone wanted to arouse doubts in me about some fixed belief, "and if I did not allow myself to be shaken but kept to my certainty—then my doing so cannot be wrong, even if only because this is just what defines a game."[3] If you fix the statement $437 + 1,912 = 2,349$ or All brothers are male or All pesticides damage the environment, then in your world no states of play are allowed in which a sister is male or $437 + 1,912 = 2,348$ or a pesticide helps the environment—such a thing is inconceivable, against the rules. No matter how many times you added a pile of 437 beans to a pile of 1,912 and counted 2,348 in the resulting pile, you would assume that you had made a mistake or that a bean had been lost.

Now look at the fundamentalist intellectual style. If you are temperamentally inclined to nail down a lot of beliefs, then there will be much about the world which you will regard as necessarily true, and which therefore cannot and need not be checked. Thus, for instance, my free-market friend P., shown empirical studies concluding that the minimum wage helps the poor, throws out the studies as misleading or cooked or otherwise invalid. And the studies concluding that the minimum wage hurts the poor just tell him what he knows must be so anyway. (Why check "All brothers are male"? What would be the point? And how could you do it?) Once I mentioned to a free-marketer that, by all standard measures, Japan's economy had outperformed America's throughout the postwar period, but that through most of the same period the Japanese government had directed the economy to an extent that would be unthinkable in America—allocating credit, keeping markets closed, telling industries what to do, and so on. My friend didn't bat an eye. He said that if Japan's economy had grown faster than America's, then the Japanese government must in fact have been less interventionist than the American government. Any appearances to the contrary had to be deceptive.

Some people are capable of clinging to a belief despite all the contrary evidence and all the ridicule in the world—sometimes admirably, sometimes not. One man, who devoted his life to arguing that the Nazis had no policy of exterminating Jews, wrote: "I get up in the morning, I go to the typewriter and write down the simplest things which have the most tremendous implications. I write about how all the historians are wrong, how the scholars and the intellectuals and the universities are all wrong and I'm right."[4] Often the true believer will resort to supernaturalism: the conviction that the absence of evidence only proves the point. Absence of evidence for miracles, goes one of the most familiar supernaturalist arguments, only shows that they *are* miracles. Absence of evidence that pornography regularly leads to violence against women, goes a more sophisticated version, only confirms the power of male supremacist society to hide the harm it does—but the harm is no less real for being hidden. Absence of evidence that the Jews control the world economy, goes a classic conspiratorial version, only shows how cunningly the Jewish network has covered its traces. When all else fails, supernaturalism is hard to beat.

When a person who is strongly attached to his fixed belief finally does drop it or exchange it for another, the changeover comes in an intellectual crisis—a time of frightening confusion or of revelatory, world-transforming experience. Imagine that you suddenly saw that your whole concept of a brother was wrong and that a female *can* be a brother. From that moment, if you met brothers, you would have to check to determine their sex. Your world would look radically different—redefined, redrawn. Many of us undergo that kind of intellectual crisis and transformation at one time or another, but it is particularly a feature of fundamentalist life (being "born again," for instance).

Whether you or I or anybody else is inclined to take seriously the possibility of being wrong is a purely personal matter, of no concern to me here—*as long as* we all obey the liberal rules that make fundamentalism safe for nonbelievers.

However, among those to whom truth is obvious, purges, jihads, crackdowns on the independent minded, and violent schisms are common—so common as to be routine. On the religious side, think of Khomeini and Rushdie, of the protests against *The Last Temptation of Christ,* of the fundamentalist Southern Baptists' crusade to squeeze moderates out of the church leadership, of Israeli fundamentalists' efforts to "oppose any manifestation of religious pluralism in Israel."[5] More brutal and sinister still, in this century, than the crusades of religious fundamentalism have been the campaigns mounted by political fundamentalists. In the Soviet Union, China, Vietnam, and many other countries, countless thousands of intellectuals and dissidents have paid for their "false" beliefs—real, imagined, or expected—with their lives. In America, the McCarthyite witch-hunts of anti-Communist fundamentalists, although kids' stuff by Communist standards, were hardly innocuous.

In other words, the relationship between fundamentalism and intellectual authoritarianism (the Fundamentalist Principle) is close. Where you find one, you usually find the other. Understanding the connection between the two is important if one wants to understand why Khomeini attacked Rushdie, and why vast numbers of people will always support similar attacks. You might think that the fundamentalist, so secure in his belief, would feel the least need to trouble others who were in error. But the reverse is true. One reason is political, another moral.

First the political reason.

Once I asked one of my hard-core free-market friends whether there would be a science of economics in a world of people who believed as he did. He said that there probably would be, but that it would be a lot simpler. Few people, if anyone, would study questions like, What can a government do to make the economy work better?—for only one answer would be possible. (In his view, government activities can no more make the economy more efficient than he could draw a three-sided square or be a sister.) Anti-drug fundamentalists have no patience for assertions that crack cocaine is not almost instantaneously addictive. To animal-rights fundamentalists, what animals want and deserve is too obvious to need checking. A leading animal-rights activist, demanding a certain amount of regular exercise for dogs used in research, told the *Washington Post* (the italics are mine): "It is not something that requires scientific proof. Everybody knows dogs don't want to sit in cages for years and years. *It's not even a question.*"[6]

Precisely. There is no question where there can be only one answer. The game of science can be played only where belief is not fixed. Where only one outcome can be legitimate, an open-ended, decentralized process is nothing more than a standing invitation to make the wrong decision. Who needs a selection process when the choice is obvious? If I believe that Bill Clinton is the only legitimate ruler, then I will see no point in having an election. If I believe that goods can

have only one "fair" price, or that everyone is entitled to an equal
amount of everything, then I will see no point in having a market.
And if I believe in the inerrancy of the Bible's account of creation,
then I will see no point in evolutionary biology—which will, in fact,
look both unnecessary and dangerous.

That is why fundamentalism feuds with democracy. In January
1989, fundamentalist Christians in Arizona got the state Republican
party to adopt a resolution saying that the Constitution created "a
republic based upon the 'absolute laws' [i.e., final say] of the Bible,
not a democracy based on the changing whims of the people."[7]
The fundamentalist preacher and former presidential candidate Pat
Robertson once said: "The Constitution of the United States is a
marvelous document for self-government by a Christian people. But
the minute you turn the document into the hands of non-Christian
people and atheist people, they can use it to destroy the very founda-
tions of our society. And that's what's happening."[8] Robertson was
right. Democracy never guarantees any particular outcome, Christian
or otherwise. And neither does liberal science. Which is why fundamentalists are generally enemies of both.

But here is a problem: if not a science game, what? One way or
another, every community has to confront that signal problem—
people disagree and you must have a way to decide who is right.
Well, if you can't fix the process, then fix the outcome. Band together
with others like mind and organize your group around a set of
fixed beliefs: a text that embodies your knowledge. The group's members hold firm to the common beliefs and, through them, to each
other. When a dispute comes up (does the earth revolve around the
sun or the sun around the earth?), members of the community go
to the text, which is treated as superhuman and changeless (like
Plato's forms). To keep the community together, the first priority is
to defend the central text. "The definition of Judaism was set down
ages ago by the Halakha," one Orthodox Israeli Jew said. "We can't
let it disappear."[9] "It would be better," William Jennings Bryan once
said, "to destroy every other book ever written, and save just the first
three verses of Genesis."[10] The text isn't the only way of settling
disagreements and answering open questions, but it is the supreme

way: it has the final say. The orthodox can do science—but only up to the point where it impinges on the fixed text. In the fall of 1987, at the First International Conference on Scientific Miracles of the Koran and Sunnah (held in Pakistan), one speaker said, "If there is a contradiction between a definitive [Koranic] text and conjectural science, then the scientific theory is refuted."[11]

The religious orthodox are not, of course, the only fundamentalists with Bibles. Yuri P. Maltsev, an economist who emigrated from the old Soviet Union, has said that even after glasnost many Soviet economists continued to regard Marx and Lenin as the source of all economic knowledge. In the days of the Communists, reliance on the Marxist texts so permeated Soviet life that Maltsev's sister, an immunologist performing research on AIDS, felt obliged to cite Marx and Lenin to support her findings. Maltsev himself emigrated largely because he was frustrated and bored by knowing the results of his research in advance. "It's like medieval Europe," he said, "when all thinking was under religious dressing. Students everywhere are indoctrinated with this Marxism." Even if you don't believe it, you may not know what to substitute for it: "The real constraint is that starting from childhood, in kindergarten, people are absolutely deprived of anything else besides Marx and Lenin. The soil of their mind would not be receptive to other seeds." I asked Maltsev whether genuine liberal science could be broadly established in what was then the Soviet Union. "I'm afraid it will take years and years," he said. Establishing an error-seeking community on the rubble of intellectual authoritarianism is not easy. Guaranteed knowledge and fixed texts, like state-guaranteed jobs and fixed prices, are dependence forming. If you're used to relying on an orthodoxy and it collapses, you're likelier to go looking for a new orthodoxy than for mistakes.

"Islam contains everything," Khomeini once said. "Islam includes everything. Islam is everything."[12] He was speaking literally. In a radically fundamentalist culture, people become obsessed with their fixed beliefs and utterly dependent upon them. The world outside the text is a dark upheaval of argument and ignorance, an uproar of hypotheses that the text cannot encompass and disputes that the text cannot settle. And so the outside world is denied, and the text is assumed to answer all questions of any genuine importance. There is a problem, however: if a list of doctrinal statements is big enough to contain the answers to all important questions, it is also big enough to contain ambiguities and contradictions. Dangerous disputes will arise over the text. To settle them, the orthodox rely on a common authority, on someone whom they regard as having special powers of insight and thus special ability to sort truth from falsehood.

And so at last we reach the fundamentalist social principle: *Those who know the truth should decide who is right.* If you believe that truth is obvious, then it is obvious who should settle differences of opinion: those who know the truth. This is the fundamentalist way: rule by the right-thinking, exclusion and (if necessary) elimination of the wrong-thinking.

Please note that you need not be a hard-core fundamentalist to support the Fundamentalist Principle; for Plato, it was enough to believe that some people are wiser than others and that the wisest should sort truth from falsehood. Interestingly, the cosmopolitan Plato of 380 B.C. was incomparably more cynical than the generally sincere Iranian fundamentalist of 1989. Khomeini the true believer really believed in the Koran, whereas Plato the sophisticate made no bones about building his regime on convenient lies and cradle-to-grave brainwashing. Khomeini wanted to defend obvious truth, Plato to maintain social order and national strength. Yet the regime of Plato's Republic wound up looking eerily like the regime of Khomeini's Iran: leadership by a philosopher-ruler and a guardian class of priest-administrators; propagation of a supporting ideology complete with creation story and moral code; regulation of words, art, and even music to stave off corruption and decadent influences.

"We want music that lifts the spirit, as in marches, music that makes our youth move instead of paralyzing them, music that helps them to care about their country." Thus Khomeini, explaining why the music of Bach, Beethoven, and Verdi must be prohibited unless it "does not dull the mind."[13] Compare, "Leave us that [musical] mode that would fittingly imitate the utterances and the accents of a brave man who is engaged in warfare or any other enforced business." Thus Plato, explaining why dirges and "soft and convivial" music must be prohibited in the Republic.[14] Though the parallel is imperfect, the creepy kinship between the Platonic Republic and the Islamic one suggests a lesson: that the Fundamentalist Principle, whether empowered by zealous true believers or calculating elites, proceeds, once established, according to the remorseless logic of authoritarianism.

The authority may be a philosopher-king, a priest or pope, an ayatollah, a messianic or visionary figure, a dictator, an oracle, a council of elders, an ecclesiastical council, a political committee or politburo. Once the authority is set up, it must be jealously defended. After all, if the authority falls, how are you to know truth from falsehood? Often the rank and file are willing to defend their truth-giver even to ludicrous extremes. Among the witnesses at the Reverend Jim Bakker's trial for fraud was one "who said that he would believe Bakker even if the defrocked televangelist said he could fit [Assistant U.S. Attorney Jerry] Miller, a burly 6-foot-3-inch former college football player, into a courtroom water pitcher."[15] In North Korea, a civil engineer said that President Kim Il Sung knew better than the scientists where to build the West Sea Barrage dam. Asked how that could be possible, the engineer said: "Comrade Kim Il Sung knows every aspect of our national economy. He knows everything. Well, almost everything. And so he can guide our technicians."[16]

A knowledge industry organized under central authoritarian control can do some things very well. For instance, at least until it becomes bureaucratized (which it will, as the decisions get more complicated), it can give quick and sure answers to all sorts of questions. But it is always under pressure from the natural diversity of human opinion. Faced with the constant threat that someone will begin arguing with authority or challenging the fixed text, an orthodox society typically has only two ways to respond: by cracking up or by cracking down.

Liberal science tends to settle disagreements by trying to pull more players and more ideas into the game: maybe a new observation or idea or thinker will show the way around the impasse. If Freudian psychological theorists are unable to solve the puzzle of human consciousness, in come the neurologists, then the computer scientists, then the biochemists. Since there is no higher appeal than of each to each, the critical society of liberal science is a beehive of shifting beliefs and arguments and alliances; it breaks up and rearranges itself a million times a day. Because authority is generalized, disputes are localized. Arguments are between individuals or small groups, not between powerful bureaucratized belief states. Big arguments, like the one that afflicted the geological community of two hundred years ago, are typically disaggregated into smaller ones as people hunt for consensual ground.

An orthodox society is more likely to react to disputes by breaking up and contracting: that is, by schism. Because authority is centralized, disputes become generalized. You're either for the authority or against it. Little arguments are aggregated into bigger ones as factions emerge and lines harden. Disputes arise over who is the rightful authority, followed by turmoil, followed by a schism, followed by more turbulent cycles later on. Sometimes the process is peaceful and invigorating; often it is violent and destabilizing, as the religious wars following the Reformation showed so memorably. The threat that the community will break up into a thousand little belief groups is never far away.

There is a way to prevent schism and so keep the society from falling apart: by cracking down. Disputes over fixed beliefs are always a threat to social cohesion, because both sides are stubborn. (Just look at the fight over abortion.) One strategy for avoiding socially dangerous disputes over fixed beliefs is to try to get rid of fixed beliefs. Generally speaking, that is liberal science's approach. Another strategy is to try to get rid of disputes. Generally speaking, that is the orthodox society's approach: get rid of disputes by suppressing criticism.

After all, what if some critic starts persuading people that the common text or authority is wrong? Then a political struggle ensues, with no orderly process by which to overthrow the old or legitimize the new. The whole regime may collapse. In an orthodox community, the threat of social disintegration is never further away than the first dissenter.

So the community joins together to stigmatize dissent. All the institutions of society—schools, family, circles of friends, political organizations, churches—join in the effort to preserve the common compact of belief. In public rituals like prayer meetings and propaganda rallies, people affirm their belief and shame the unorthodox. Intellectual conformity is a social value. Sometimes tacitly, sometimes explicitly, sometimes by twisting arms or breaking them, everyone encourages everyone else not to doubt, not to criticize. The common text and common authority knit the group together. If you search for error, you endanger the peace.

An intellectual is an argument waiting to happen. Thus it is that fundamentalist societies, whether they are religious or political, Platonic or Communist or Islamic, so often punish intellectualism and institutionalize incuriosity. When I worked as a newspaper reporter in North Carolina in the early 1980s, a copy of a fundamentalist Christian list of "Don'ts for students" crossed my desk. Among the items were "DON'T exchange 'opinions' on political or social issues," "Don't discuss values," and "Don't get into classroom discussions which begin:

What would you do if . . . ?
What if . . . ?
Should we . . . ?
Do you suppose . . . ?
Do you think . . . ?
What is your opinion of . . . ?
Who should . . . ?
What might happen if . . . ?
Do you value . . . ?
Is it moral to . . . ?"

Curiosity killed the cat.

But what about the outside world? Members of an anti-critical culture find themselves and, perhaps more to the point, their children under constant criticism by nonbelievers on the outside. The very existence of nonbelievers sends a message: "Your necessary truths are false, your authority is not special, and our presence here outside your fortress will be a standing mockery of you and a temptation to your children." In a kind of social version of covering one's ears and talking loudly, the culture tries to shut out the rest of the world, with its threatening din of contrary belief—just as fundamentalist religious groups do with their separate schools and their self-imposed ghettos, and just as the Communist countries did with their closed borders and controlled presses. The center must control all channels of communication with the exterior. "Every channel, every satellite, every radio, every television ought to belong to God's people," the Pentecostal preacher Paul Crouch said on his TV show in 1988.[17] Only when all sources of criticism are either banished or controlled is the regime really safe.

But of course every radio and every television cannot "belong to God's people": the rest of the world cannot be shut out, even by a Khomeini or a Stalin. So there must be some effort to convert the outsiders or to punish them. The effort may fail, but it must be made. And the fundamentalist society cannot relax its efforts to maintain purity within. "The outgoing president of the Southern Baptist Convention says there is no room in the denomination for humanists or those who do not accept the absolute inerrancy of the Bible."[18] That statement is typical of the sorts of things one reads every day about religious fundamentalist groups. And the attitude it reflects is socially necessary. The us-versus-them mentality of fundamentalists all over the world is not the product of paranoia. It is the product of a clear understanding that central authority must be defended at all costs in an intellectual culture which has no other means to resolve its members' disagreements.

When Khomeini decreed that Rushdie must die, many people said that he was merely acting to shore up his power in Iran by pandering to his fundamentalist constituency, as though that would somehow be reassuring. (You couldn't pander to a liberal by offering to kill someone who disagreed with him.) Those people missed the point. Khomeini certainly was acting to shore up his power, but that was not all he was doing. He and his followers believed that Rushdie presented a clear and present danger to their culture. And they were right. Rushdie questioned the truth of their text and mocked their authority, and in so doing he took a pickax to the foundation of their society—even to the meaning, for fundamentalist Muslims, of objective truth itself. They had not actually read Rushdie's book— just as the movie protesters had not actually seen *The Last Temptation of Christ*. But they didn't have to read the book; their society was threatened by the very existence of such a challenge. And the threat they perceived was real. Intellectual liberalism, by its very nature, denies the legitimacy of any fixed truth or special authority, even in principle. Many people spoke of the Rushdie affair as a "clash of cultures," which it was. But more precisely it was a clash of political systems. When liberals looked at Rushdie, they saw a member of an international critical community going about his business. When fundamentalist Muslims looked at him, they saw, so to speak, a regicide—a man bent on overthrowing rightful Islamic authority and so on tearing apart Islamic society.

And so to call the fundamentalists nutty or irrational does them a profound injustice. When fundamentalist communities rise in rage against heresy of whatever sort, when they shake their fists and draw their knives against the imperialism of liberal science, they are acting in genuine self-defense. They are acting to stave off social and political chaos. That is what makes them so dangerous.

The other connection between fundamentalism and the centralized control of knowledge is moral.

We journalists learn from our daily business what no school can properly teach: just because someone is as smart and as well-intentioned as I am does not mean that he and I will reach the same conclusions. I had an acquaintance—a perfectly sane man—who believed that his spiritual guide regularly "channeled" a five-hundred-year-old entity called Saint Germaine. He (my acquaintance, not Saint Germaine) also liked to talk about a delegation of Arcturians he knew who lived in a group house in Los Angeles. Another man I met, who is no crazier than I am, once told me matter-of-factly that spirits sometimes knocked the pictures off the walls in his house. I remember reading about a preacher who put the body of his recently departed mother in a freezer and posted his flock outside to hold a prayer vigil, promising that on the seventh day she would rise again. (I never found out whether she did.) The more I get around, the more deeply I am impressed that the gardens of human belief flower more exotically than any in nature.

To a skeptic, knowledge is elusive and mistakenness the inescapable human condition. My world is a place buzzing with interpreters of an ornery reality which is always trying to trip them up. And to me the buzz is a joyful sound. When an experiment seemed to show conclusively that there are only three basic families of fundamental particles, one physicist said, "For me it's very disappointing. For it means that there are no new particles to find."[19] I admire this man's spirit. If there is a Being somewhere who is above error, before whom all reality is spread in static clarity, I feel sorry for Him. I believe God would want to have a mistake to hunt for.

A fundamentalist would not feel that way, for a fundamentalist is one to whom truth about the external world is obvious. Is it not obvious, after all, that a brother is a male? that $437 + 1,912 = 2,349$? that government can only make us poorer? In 1964 Barry Goldwater's presidential campaign rallied under the slogan: "In your heart you know he's right." That is the most revealing fundamentalist slogan I've ever heard. Goldwater's seven words speak volumes about the morality of the Fundamentalist Principle.

To a hard-core fundamentalist, there is one clear truth in the world and many liars. The other side is not merely wrong, it is *lying*. That is why, to anti-abortion fundamentalists, the supporters of abortion favor not just killing but murder: pro-choicers want to allow premeditated killing of what they themselves know to be human beings. "So convinced are the evangelicals of the rightness of their cause," Garry Wills wrote of some anti-abortion activists he interviewed, "that they tend to see nothing but evil intent in opposition to them."[20] Just as blindly, pro-choice fundamentalists often insist that pro-lifers really don't believe that a fetus is a human being—how could they? Rather, the purported concern for the fetus must be a mask, a ruse, camouflaging the anti-abortionists' real crusade to repeal women's rights and repress nonprocreative sex. Right-wing political fundamentalists in America, including many conservatives in Washington, insist that their liberal opponents are knowingly out to hurt the country, and so are traitorous or at best unpatriotic. Left-wing political fundamentalists insist that their conservative opponents deliberately want to starve the poor or blow up the planet. For if truth is obvious, then if you don't see it you must be crazy, stupid, or acting in bad faith. The very best you can say about people who deny obvious truth is that they are (as my free-market friend put it) "willfully naive." In your heart, you know we're right.

Paul, who at first persecuted Jesus's cause with as much zeal as he later championed it, was one of the most influential of all the fundamentalists. It was he who wrote this extraordinary statement of the fundamentalist creed: "For the wrath of God is revealed from heaven against all ungodliness and wickedness of men who by their wickedness suppress the truth. For what can be known about God is plain to them, because God has shown it to them. Ever since the creation of the world his invisible nature, namely, his eternal power and deity, has been clearly perceived in the things that have been made. So they are without excuse."[21]

Upon that chilling Pauline declaration and others like it stand many centuries of killing, torture, and repression of people who perversely, "by their wickedness," denied evident truth. Certainly, there can be no right to say what is false and what you know is false. Even ignorance of evident truth—being "willfully naive"—is hard to excuse. Remember Plato: it is not right, he had said, "to speak as having knowledge about things one does not know," for "opinions divorced from knowledge are ugly things." Ugly, yes, and dangerous too: not only repulsive but also likely to steer people away from the salving light of truth, the truth to which any good and functional society must hold.

From holding that someone who disagrees with you cannot be of good sense or good conscience to holding that such a person deserves censure or punishment is a very short step. Not all of the people who could take that step actually do so. But the temptation is always strong. From a hard-core fundamentalist's point of view, a dissenter is not just someone who endangers the social order; he is someone who does so in order to spread lies. And it is certainly immoral to protect liars. Salman Rushdie was not only an unbeliever but a slanderer and a hatemonger, a man knowingly out to smear Muhammad. How could one contemplate *not* punishing such a person?

Before the skeptical revolution and the rise of liberal science, the destruction of the unorthodox was widely seen as an unpleasant but principled and necessary task. It not only needed to be done, it *ought* to be done. ("For what can be known about God is plain to them, because God has shown it to them. So they are without excuse.") The British historian Conrad Russell, in his discussion of the burning of heretics under Queen Mary I in the mid-1500s, wrote:

> It should be remembered . . . that most of the people who were burned believed in the burning of heretics as firmly as most of the Marian bishops. . . . Contemporary objections, though common, were not based on the principle that heretics should not be burned: they were based, either on the assumption that the people who were burned were not heretics, or simply on a humanitarian or expedient readiness to ignore principle.[22]

This is the morality of the Fundamentalist Principle: he who would deny evident truth should be punished. Wherever the believers in the Fundamentalist Principle get the upper hand, they strive restlessly and untiringly to suppress diversity of opinion, and they do so not simply out of cynicism or power lust, but, on the contrary, out of the purest and most principled of motives.

In its full-blown modern form, totalitarianism is relatively new. But the *idea* of totalitarianism, that to believe incorrectly is a crime, is hardly an innovation. It is, indeed, a logical outgrowth of hard-line fundamentalism. What is new is only the extent to which Communist governments extended the totalitarian idea, using means that were not available to the Inquisition—just as the racist idea, that to be of the wrong kind is a crime, is ancient, but its application in this century under the Nazis crossed a new threshold of horror. We read that in Communist China "there have been instances, even very recently, in which lectures in the natural sciences have been banned on political grounds."[23] We read of the Soviet dissident Andrei Amalrik, who was told in 1960 that his university dissertation was brilliant but that its conclusion, that Normans as well as Slavs influenced early Russian culture, contradicted the official position and was politically unacceptable; for his activities as a dissident, he was harassed, imprisoned in Siberia, abused, and at last expelled.[24] (The Soviet use of psychiatry against dissidents seems less odd when you remember that, to a committed fundamentalist, someone who does not see evident truth must be crazy if he is not stupid or evil.) In principle, that sort of behavior is basically no different from the Inquisition's confinement of Galileo and its command that he renounce Copernicanism. Indeed, the principle that to believe incorrectly is a crime (if you like, a sin) has for centuries been a doctrinal mainstay of a number of religions, among them Christianity. True, fundamentalism need not lead to genuine totalitarianism, which is the assertion of central power over truth with absolute ruthlessness and for the sake of power itself. However, where the Fundamentalist Principle holds sway, no one can feel completely safe to err.

I find the suppression of criticism repugnant, even within voluntary associations (churches, for instance) whose legal right to engage in it I will ardently defend. If you do not happen to share my revulsion, I draw your attention to the practical shortcomings of orthodox societies. Letting colonels or commissars or cardinals decide which ideas are worthy is a bad way to stay in touch with reality. According to Maltsev, the Soviets had no usable statistics on their service economy, and thus no reliable measure of their gross national product, because their dogma defined as nonproductive all labor that performs services instead of making goods. Moreover, regimes that fear criticism find that people trained to think scientifically—people like Fang Lizhi in China and Andrei Sakharov in the old Soviet Union—are likely to become dangerous dissidents, because science teaches us to doubt and criticize. As everyone knows by now, anti-critical societies tend to be narrow, rigid, and backward. They cannot easily get rid of old ideas, they cannot readily produce new ideas, and when they do produce new ideas they cannot efficiently check them. They use their intellectual resources counterproductively or clumsily or not at all.

Worse yet, they wind up settling differences of opinion by punishing weak people rather than weak ideas. Plato believed that empowering a wise central authority was the surest way to make certain that truth prevailed over nonsense. What he failed to realize—or maybe did realize but did not say—was that in an authoritarian intellectual regime the advantage goes to the people with the most troops, not the people with the keenest critical eyes. "Truth" is built on the ruined careers and broken bodies and enforced silence of the unorthodox.

Creed wars will never end completely, even within societies whose ethic is predominantly liberal. The game of science can only be played in the open spaces between fixed beliefs; and unless a time comes when we all share the same feelings and deep preferences, we will have to settle some disputes (about abortion, for instance) the old-fashioned way—by politics, and sometimes by force. All of that I grant you. But liberal science can make our intellectual problems more manageable and less dangerous. In an imperfect world, the best insurance we have against truth's being politicized is to put no one in particular in charge of it. That is the lesson which—as I will now try to show—the new enemies of liberal science, the egalitarians and humanitarians, are flouting.

5

The Humanitarian Threat

"The liberation of the human mind," H. L. Mencken once wrote, "has been best furthered by gay fellows who heaved dead cats into sanctuaries and then went roistering down the highways of the world, proving to all men that doubt, after all, was safe—that the god in the sanctuary was a fraud. One horse-laugh is worth ten thousand syllogisms."

When I think of the towering Plato and the brooding Paul, with their horror of error and their burning brilliance, I like to think next of Mencken—Mencken the rambunctious heaver of dead cats, the horse-laugher, the irrepressible American skeptic. Mencken stood in a great American tradition: a tradition of doubt and inquiry and rowdy reformulation of truth. "All of my work hangs together, once the main ideas under it are discerned," he said. "These ideas are chiefly of a skeptical character. I believe that nothing is unconditionally true, and hence I am opposed to every statement of positive truth and every man who states it." No final say—that was Mencken, down to the soles of his feet.

But there is another America, too—an America of herdthink, of intolerance. Even in this country of sharp-eyed mistrust of authority, the pressure on liberal inquiry is constant and can never be ignored. One must press back continually—and especially recently.

The trouble with talking so much about the threat to liberal science from the Khomeinis and Communists of the world is that in some ways they are the least of our problems. Americans have enough Menckenian instinct in their guts to be frightened by overt intellectual authoritarianism, even if they don't always precisely understand the nature of the threat. It is true that the response to Khomeini's attack on Rushdie was tepid and incoherent. But it is also true that Americans hated what Khomeini's regime stood for. That, in itself, was a pretty good backstop against the worst kind of retreat. Americans typically have no intellectually elegant answer to the challenge from hard-core religious fundamentalists in the Islamic countries or here at home, but they do *feel* that in religious fundamentalism lurks a kind of dangerous alienness. They know viscerally that hard-core fundamentalism is a different kind of animal from garden-variety Episcopalianism. They can sniff the authoritarian goods inside the spiritual wrapping. That may not always be good enough, but when push comes to shove it is something.

Old-fashioned religious fundamentalism is a real and important threat to intellectual liberalism in America. Here, as I have been at such great pains to show, the nature of the danger is not religious; it is fundamentalist. However, I don't think the old-fashioned religious brand of intellectual authoritarianism is worth losing sleep over in this country right now. The war whoops of Khomeini and his raging supporters have awakened many snoozing Westerners to the fact that tens or hundreds of millions of people really do detest liberalism; we can thank the Islamic fundamentalists for the reminder that totalitarianism never leaves us alone. At home, religious fundamentalism is a minority interest, not very powerful—weak enough, in fact, to be treated with arrogance and contempt by the intellectual establishment when it is worthy instead of respectful enmity. Liberals need to keep an eye on the religious authoritarians. Eternal vigilance is the price of science. But where religious true believers are concerned, at any rate, we are pretty vigilant. The greater threat lies in our letting down our guard against ourselves: in high-mindedly embracing authoritarianism in the name of fairness and compassion, as the Marxists did. Having been at last rousted out of politics and economics by the disaster of communism, the authoritarian Rasputin has now come calling on liberal science, and he already has his foot in the door.

To begin with, I should be clear about what I mean by intellectual egalitarianism. In one sense, liberal science is as egalitarian as any system could be: where the game of science is properly played, no one is granted personal authority simply because of who he happens to be—period. The rules apply to everybody. It is quite true that for most of history (and not just in the West) women, blacks, and others were denied equal access to the intellectual and scientific establishment, as they were denied equal access to so much else. But that represents not the failure of liberalism but the failure to embrace it. To renounce liberal science because the society in which it was embedded tended to shut out women is as silly as it would have been to renounce democracy in 1910 because women were not allowed to vote. Science, when it works the way it is supposed to, is an equal-opportunity knowledge-maker.

But that is very different—radically, fundamentally different—from being an equal-*results* knowledge-maker. Some people who understand the difference clamor for equal results—for instance, people on the political left who demand an equal place in the canon of knowledge for minority groups' points of view. Many more people, however, simply misunderstand. They don't realize that there is a wide gulf between equal access to a knowledge-making system and equal results. Their misunderstanding has the potential for grave consequences.

One of the most troubling examples I know is *Edwards v. Aguillard*. The reason the case is so troubling is that its attack on intellectual liberalism was subscribed to by two justices of the U.S. Supreme Court. The state of Louisiana had passed a statute (the Balanced Treatment for Creation-Science and Evolution-Science in Public School Instruction Act) requiring that wherever in public schools the theory of evolution was taught, "scientific creationism" was to be taught along with it. The act did not require that either one be taught; only that if one was, so must be the other. The bill's sponsors felt that students were being indoctrinated with one (disputed) view of how humanity came to be; they thus demanded that the evidence on both sides be presented if the subject were to be broached. They said that they were trying to ensure balance, not enforce religion. One state senator stressed that to teach religion in disguise was not his intent: "My intent is to see to it that our textbooks are not censored."

In 1987 the Supreme Court struck down the law as unconstitutional. But Justice Antonin Scalia, one of the brightest judges on the American bench, strongly dissented; he was joined by the chief justice, William Rehnquist. The disturbing thing was that Scalia's dissent was aimed straight at what liberal intellectual standards are all about. And it is a mark of the egalitarian fallacy's seductiveness that the conservative Scalia and the still more conservative Rehnquist tumbled right into bed with the left-wing people who say that to insist on science is to oppress minority traditions. Of course, Rehnquist and Scalia were only two justices among nine; but things change. As one supporter of the Louisiana law remarked, there would be time enough to try again. "With four justices approaching age 80, the court won't stay the same forever."[1]

Leave to one side the constitutional questions involved. (Scalia argued that the law was of secular rather than religious intent and so did not fail the established test of constitutionality.) The question of constitutionality was central to the Court, but not to the egalitarian attack. What *was* central was the background view of knowledge which informed Scalia's dissent: that the Louisiana legislature was seeking to ensure academic freedom, and that academic freedom could be advanced by requiring that evidence for all beliefs, or at least more than one, be presented. It is important to see that you could apply that argument to secular beliefs just as easily as to religious ones. If states began passing laws requiring equal time for astrology— and it's a wonder they haven't—Scalia's egalitarian view of knowledge would say they were doing the fair thing. Scalia said that the evidence for evolution was not conclusive, and that the law's supporters had presented testimony that creationism had scientific support. Therefore throwing out a state's attempt to give both sides a hearing, he said, was "illiberal." "In this case," he said, "it seems to me the Court's position is the repressive one."

That, of course, is just what the complaints from the left assert: the Western view of objective knowledge and the scientific order built upon it are both "repressive." The egalitarian line of thinking holds that, since any standard for truth is biased and political, no one's standard should get special privileges, but rather all should be

equal; and these days the argument often adds that, since some views
have been squashed under the boot of Eurocentric domination (or,
for that matter, secular humanist domination), the claims of repressed
minority groups should be more equal than others.

For instance, "The monocultural perspective of traditional American education *restricts the scope of knowledge*" (my italics). That is
from the report by New York State's 1989 task force on minorities
and education.[2] The quotation continues with, "It acts as a constraint
on the critical thinking of African American, Asian American, Native
American, and Puerto Rican/Latino youth because of its hidden
assumptions of 'white supremacy' and 'white nationalism.' " Only the
particulars are left-wing. The charge itself—that "the monocultural
perspective of traditional American education restricts the scope of
knowledge"—could just as easily have come from the creationist
right. The bill of particulars might just as easily have read, "It acts
as a constraint on the critical thinking of American youth because of
its hidden assumptions of 'Darwinist supremacy' and 'secular
humanism.' " Either way, the argument is the same: the establishment's view of what the "facts" are and how to find them has excluded
someone, and the way to ensure intellectual freedom (broaden "the
scope of knowledge") is to rewrite the texts so as to let that someone
in. "A lot of black people have been devastated by the assumption
that black people never did anything, and when we did do anything
there were other races involved in it," one Rutgers University teacher
said.[3] Similarly, some fundamentalist Christians have been devastated
by the assumption that the Bible is outmoded as an account of human
creation, and some Christian Scientists have been devastated by the
rejection of their ideas about healing. At bottom, the complaint is
the same.

That the left-wing and right-wing intellectual egalitarians have so
far failed to make common cause is a function merely of expediency,
not principle. It reflects, I suppose, that their hatred for each other
exceeds their commitment to the "equal rights" of oppressed minorities. Creationists tend to believe unapologetically in the superiority
of Christendom to other cultures. Multiculturalists tend to see fundamentalist Christians as oppressors of women, gays, and so on. As is

so often the case with egalitarian activists, they support equality for everybody, except people who don't share their political agenda. That multiculturalists don't fight for the inclusion of fundamentalist Christian viewpoints in high school and college classrooms is, no doubt, understandable. But it must qualify as one of our day's great hypocrisies that those self-appointed guardians of "oppressed-minority viewpoints" have nothing to say in defense of one of America's own "traditional" minority cultures, namely the religious fundamentalists.

That, however, is a minor point. What about the major point? What about the charge that one person's knowledge is another's repression? What is intellectual freedom in a liberal truth-seeking regime? Is it repressive or unfair to insist that conventional science is *the* standard for respectable knowledge?

On its face Scalia's argument was plausible, especially since it appeals to one of Americans' most laudable principles, namely the principle of political equality. There is no doubt that the argument is impelled by decency. But in fact it is very dangerous. It cuts out, with a surgeon's precision, the heart of a peculiar and subtle distinction on which all of Western intellectual life—I do not exaggerate—depends. That distinction is as follows:

To believe incorrectly is never a crime, *but simply to believe is never to have knowledge.*

In other words, liberal science does not restrict belief, *but it does restrict knowledge.* It absolutely protects freedom of belief and speech, but it absolutely *denies* freedom of knowledge: in liberal science, there is positively *no* right to have one's opinions, however heartfelt, taken seriously as knowledge. Just the contrary: liberal science is nothing other than a selection process whose mission is to test beliefs and reject the ones that fail. A liberal intellectual regime says that if you want to believe the moon is made of green cheese, fine. But if you want your belief recognized as knowledge, there are things you must *do.* You must run your belief through the science game for checking. And if your belief is a loser, it will *not* be included in the science texts. It probably won't even be taken seriously by most respectable intellectuals. In a liberal society, knowledge—not belief—is the rolling critical consensus of a decentralized community of checkers, *and it is nothing else*. That is so, not by the power of law, but by the deeper power of a common liberal morality.

Of course, if your belief is rejected by the critical consensus, *you* are free to reject the consensus and keep believing. That's freedom of belief. But you are not entitled to expect that your belief will be taught to schoolchildren or accepted by the intellectual establishment *as knowledge*.[4] Any school curriculum is necessarily restrictive. It cannot *not* be restrictive. My point is that the right way to set a curriculum is to insist that it teach knowledge, and that this knowledge should consist only of claims which have been thoroughly checked by no person (or group) in particular. We should never teach anything as knowledge because it serves someone's political needs. We should teach only what has checked out.

The Louisiana legislators, with Scalia's nod of approval, wanted to ensure academic freedom by requiring that evidence for both sides of a disputed issue be presented to students. Sounds fair enough. Indeed, as I've mentioned, Ronald Reagan himself endorsed the principle of equal time for creationism, and one poll found that three-fourths of the American public joined him. But academic freedom consists in freedom to doubt, to inquire, to check, and to believe as you like. It does *not* consist in the freedom of one party or another to reset the rules for inquiry or checking. Someone who wants to insist that the theory of relativity is false and that some other theory is true is, of course, entitled to do so; but passing laws or using intimidation to make teachers (or anyone else) take him seriously has nothing to do with the freedom to inquire. It has to do with the centralized regulation of knowledge. If the consensus of critical checkers holds that evolution checks out but creationism does not, and clearly it does hold this, then *that* is our knowledge on the subject.

And who decides what the critical consensus actually is? The critical society does, arguing about itself. That is why scholars spend so much time and energy "surveying the literature" (i.e., assessing the consensus so far). Then they argue about their assessments. The process is long and arduous, but there you are. Academic freedom would be trampled instead of advanced by, say, requiring that state-financed universities put creationists on their biology faculties or give Afrocentrists rebuttal space in their journals. When a state legislature or a curriculum committee or any other political body decrees that anything in particular is, or has equal claim to be, our knowledge, it wrests control over truth from the liberal community of checkers and places it in the hands of central political authorities.

And *that* is illiberal. If the principle is ever established that political bodies can say what our knowledge is or is not, or which ideas are worth taking seriously, then watch out. Everyone with an opinion would be busy lobbying legislatures for equal-time laws, demanding that biology books describe prayer as an alternative treatment for cancer, picketing universities for astrology departments, suing journals for rebuttal space, demonstrating for proportionate representation in footnote citations. We would find ourselves in a world where knowledge was made by voting and agitating. Then we really would find ourselves living Bertrand Russell's nightmare, where "the lunatic who believes that he is a poached egg is to be condemned solely on the ground that he is in the minority." In that case, those of us who believe in science had better hope that we can persuade a majority and round up a quorum—and whether we can do so is not at all clear on issues like astrology.

One cannot overemphasize: intellectual liberalism is not intellectual majoritarianism or egalitarianism. You do not have a claim to knowledge either because 51 percent of the public agrees with you or because your "group" was historically left out; you have a claim to knowledge only to the extent that your opinion still stands up after prolonged exposure to withering public testing. Now, it is true that when we talk about knowledge's being a scientific consensus we are talking about a majority of scientists. But we are not talking about a *mere* majority. For a theory to go into a textbook as knowledge, it does not need the unanimity of checkers' assent, but it does need far more than a bare majority's. It should be generally recognized as having stood up better than any competitor to most of the tests that various critical debunkers have tried. Today it is possible that a majority of climatologists believe that global warming is a fact (one can't say for sure, since scientists don't vote on these things), but global warming is far from well enough established to be presented as fact in textbooks. The point extends beyond natural science. The critical consensus of historians is that many minority groups did not make much of a contribution to the writing of the Constitution. Attempting to find a role for them and install them in the textbooks may make some people feel better. But doing so would betray the community of critical checkers. It would also lead to factional warfare as other political groups took up the cry and demanded *their* share. If, on grounds of equality, the radical Afrocentrists win equal time for their claim that the ancient Egyptians were black Africans or that the Greeks stole their learning from Africa, then the creationists, astrologists, Christian Scientists, white supremacists, and many others will follow close behind. Because space and time in textbooks and classrooms are limited, each of those groups will make demands at the expense of others. And that is how creed wars begin.

For various minorities, the answer is to do just what many black and feminist historians are doing, namely to propose new hypotheses about the role of, say, blacks and women in American history. But only *after* those hypotheses have stood up to extensive checking, only *after* each has convinced each, is it time to rewrite the texts. The checking process often takes years. So be it. The process often rules against someone whose cause seems sympathetic. So be it. All other paths to knowledge lead to creed wars. And the attempt to intimidate would-be debunkers by calling them "racist" or "sexist" or whatever is nothing but an attempt to replace science with political muscle.

Further, only *after* an idea has survived checking is it deserving of respect. Not long ago, I heard an activist say at a public meeting that her opinion deserved at least respect. The audience gave her a big round of applause. But she and they had it backwards. Respect was the most, not the least, that she could have demanded for her opinion. Except insofar as an opinion earns its stripes in the science game, it is entitled to no respect whatever. This point matters, because respectability is the coin in which liberal science rewards ideas that are duly put up for checking and pass the test. You may not get rich by being shown to be right, you may not even become famous, and you almost certainly will not be loved; but you will be paid in the specie of respectability. That is why it is so important that creationists and alien-watchers and radical Afrocentrists and white supremacists be granted every entitlement to speak but no entitlement to have their opinions respected. They should expect, if they scoff at the rules by which the game of science is played, to have their beliefs scoffed at; they should expect, if for any reason (including minority status) they refuse to submit their ideas for checking by public criticism, that their opinions will be ignored or ridiculed—and rightly so. Respect is no opinion's birthright. *People,* yes, are entitled to a certain degree of basic respect by dint of being human. But to grant any such claim to ideas is to raid the treasury of science and throw its capital to the winds.

Let us remember, then, that the proposition "We must all respect others' beliefs" is nowhere near as innocent as it sounds. If it is enshrined in policies or practices giving "rights" to minority opinions, the damage it causes is immediate and severe. Liberal science cannot exert discipline if it cannot use its tool of marginalization to drive unsupported or bogus beliefs from the agenda. When you pass laws requiring equal time for somebody's excluded belief, you effectively *make marginalization illegal.* You say, "In our society, a belief is respectable—and will be taught and treated respectfully—if the politically powerful say it is." Once you have said that, you face a very stark choice. You can open the textbooks only to those "oppressed" beliefs whose proponents have political pull. Or you can take the principled egalitarian position, and open the books and the schools to *all* sincere beliefs. If you do the former, then you have replaced science with power politics. If you do the latter, then you have no principled choice but to teach, for example, "Holocaust revisionism" (the claim that the Holocaust didn't happen) as an "alternative theory" held by an "excluded minority"—which means, in practice, not teaching twentieth-century history at all. Either way, you have taken in hand silly and even execrable opinions and ushered them from the fringes of debate to the very center. At a single stroke, you have disabled liberal society's mechanism for marginalizing foolish ideas, and you have sent those ideas straight to the top of the social agenda with a safe-conduct.

Is the liberal standard for respectability fair? That, really, is the big question today. If you believe that a society is just only when it delivers more or less equal outcomes, you will think liberalism is unfair. You will insist on admitting everyone's belief into respectability as knowledge. Or at least you will insist on admitting the beliefs of people whom you regard as oppressed—affirmative action for knowledge. Personally, I cannot think of anything good about that kind of standard for knowledge. It is bound to lead to fights over who gets what. Groups will appoint leaders, and leaders will negotiate, and when negotiations break down schism or intellectual warfare will ensue; or if negotiations are successful, then certain beliefs will be locked in place by delicate compromise, and a knowledge-making system whose greatest virtue is its adaptiveness will turn sclerotic.

As knowledge-making regimes go, nothing is as successful or as respectful of diversity or as humane as liberal science. The trouble is that liberal science often does not look very humane. It uses sticks as well as carrots. The carrots are the respectability, frequent use, and public credit that it bestows on the opinions that it validates; the sticks are the disrespect and the silent treatment that it inflicts on the opinions that fail. Those sticks are nonviolent, true. But it is unconscionable not to admit that denying respectability is a very serious matter indeed. It causes pain and outrage—outrage which Scalia's humane impulses reached out to in *Edwards v. Aguillard.* Here is where the door opens to the most formidable attack on the liberal science—the humanitarian attack.

"Well," goes the argument, "we must, it appears, have intellectual standards. But what should our standards be? Obviously it is desirable to have standards that minimize pain. And a lot of beliefs cause pain (that is, they hurt people's feelings). Racist beliefs cause pain. Anti-Semitic and sexist and homophobic beliefs cause pain. So do anti-

American and anti-religious beliefs. So do beliefs which proclaim one
ethnic group or culture to be better than another, or different from
others in some way which carries social disapproval. If we're going
to have a social system for weeding out beliefs, it should start by
weeding out beliefs which cause pain. Thus it should weed out racist
and anti-Semitic and ethnocentric and sexist beliefs. The first criterion
for sorting worthy from unworthy beliefs should be: Cause no pain,
and allow none to be caused—especially not to the politically vulnerable. Intellectuals should be like doctors. They should first do no
harm."

The empathetic spirit from which that line of thinking springs is
admirable. But the principle to which it leads is nothing but dreadful.
The right principle, and the only one consonant with liberal science,
is, Cause no pain solely in order to hurt. The wrong principle, but
the one that has increasingly taken the place of the right one, is,
Allow no pain to be caused.

The social system does not and never can exist which allows no
harm to come to anybody. Conflict of impulse and desire is an
inescapable fact of human existence, and where there is conflict there
will always be losers and wounds. Utopian systems premised on a
world of loving harmony—communism, for instance—fail because
in the attempt to obliterate conflict they obliterate freedom. The chore
of a social regime is not to obliterate conflict but to manage it, so as
to put it to good use while causing a minimum of hurt and abuse.
Liberal systems, although far from perfect, have at least two great
advantages: they can channel conflict rather than obliterate it, and
they give a certain degree of protection from centrally administered
abuse. The liberal intellectual system is no exception. It causes pain
to people whose views are criticized, still more to those whose views
fail to check out and so are rejected. But there are two important
consolations. First, no one gets to run the system to his own advantage
or stay in charge for long. Whatever you can do to me, I can do to
you. Those who are criticized may give as good as they get. Second,
the books are never closed, and the game is never over. Sometimes
rejected ideas (continental drift, for one) make sensational comebacks.

Humanitarians, though, remain unsatisfied. Their hope, which is no less appealing for being futile, is that somehow the harm can be prevented in the first place. Their worry is that the harm may emanate in two directions, one social and the other individual.

Social harm accrues to society as a whole from the spread of bad ideas; held to be especially vulnerable are minorities or groups seen as lacking power. "AIDS comes from homosexuals," "Jews fabricated the Holocaust," "Blacks are less intelligent than whites"—those ideas and others like them can do real mischief.

Though the special concern for minorities as groups is a new twist, this argument is an old and highly principled one. It was used, in all good conscience, by the Inquisition. The heretic, in those days, endangered the peace and stability of the whole society by challenging the rightful authority of the Church. The Inquisition was a policing action. But by its own lights it was a humanitarian action, too. The heretic endangered the faith of believers, and so threatened to drag others with him to an eternity of suffering in perdition; not least of all, he threw away his own soul. To allow such a person to destroy souls seemed at least as indecent as allowing racist hate speech seems today. "It is an error to think of the persecution of heretics as being forced by the Church upon unwilling or indifferent laity. The heretic was an unpopular person in the Middle Ages. There are, in fact, instances in the late eleventh century and early twelfth century of heretics being lynched by an infuriated mob, who regarded the clergy as too lenient."[5] If you cared about the good of society and about the souls of your neighbors and friends, then you believed that the Inquisition's mission was at bottom humane, even if the inquisitorial methods sometimes were not.

Humane motives, however, could not save the Inquisition from the same problem that faces humanitarians today: although allowing mistakes is risky, suppressing them is much riskier, because then a "mistake" becomes whatever it is that the authorities don't like to hear. Suppressing offensiveness, too, comes at a high cost, since offensiveness is not the same thing as wrongness—often just the contrary. Sometimes patently "offensive" verbiage turns out to be telling the unpopular truth. As I am hardly the first to point out, practically all knowledge of any importance began as a statement which offended someone. "All the durable truths that have come into the world within historic times," said Mencken, "have been opposed as bitterly as if they were so many waves of smallpox." Many people were appalled by the notion that the earth was not at the center of the universe (to say so was hate speech—hateful of God), many other people by the proposition that man was created last rather than first, and still others by the exploding of the common "knowledge" that white people were inherently more intelligent than people of all other races.

Will someone's belief, if accepted, destroy society? Maybe. But more likely not. "Throughout history, scientists have been urged to suppress their views about nature for the sake of the public welfare," wrote David Hull. That the solar system is heliocentric, that species evolve, that genes influence mental traits—at one time or another people feared that those ideas and many others would destroy society if they became widely accepted. "Thus far, however, those who have urged the suppression of new views for the 'good of the people' have underestimated the ability of both societies and individual people to survive successive challenges to their conceptions of the world and how it works."[6] So often have those who warned us about "dangerous" ideas been wrong, and so often have they abused whatever restraining power they possessed, that I have no hesitation in saying: it is better in every case to let critical public inquiry run its course than to try to protect society from it. If we have anything to learn from the progress of knowledge in the last few centuries, it is that to Peirce's injunction, "Do not block the way of inquiry," must be added, "And by no means should inquiry be blocked to 'save' society."

The other, and much newer, strand of intellectual humanitarianism is intuitively more appealing and emotionally harder to resist. It says that wrongheaded opinions and harsh words are hurtful, if not necessarily to society as a whole, then to *individuals*. And here liberal science has been put squarely on the defensive, for the first time in more than a hundred years; for here you have, not the cold-blooded public censor raising bureaucratic objections on behalf of "society," but an identifiable person saying "*I* am hurt" and speaking for his own dignity. In today's world the second kind of claim, like all human-rights claims, seems compelling. Facing it means owning up to the truth about knowledge and about the system which best produces it.

So let us be frank, once and for all: creating knowledge is painful, for the same reason that it can also be exhilarating. Knowledge does not come free to any of us; we have to suffer for it. We have to stand naked before the court of critical checkers and watch our most cherished beliefs come under fire. Sometimes we have to watch while our notion of evident truth gets tossed in the gutter. Sometimes we feel we are treated rudely, even viciously. As others prod and test and criticize our ideas, we feel angry, hurt, embarrassed.

We would all like to think that knowledge could be separated from hurt. We would all like to think that painful but useful and thus "legitimate" criticism is objectively distinguishable from criticism which is merely ugly and hurtful. Surely criticism is one thing, and "Hitler should have finished the job" is another. But what we would like to think is not so: the only such distinction is in the eye of the beholder. The fact is that even the most "scientific" criticism can be horribly hurtful, devastatingly so. The physicist Ludwig Boltzmann was so depressed by the harshness of F. W. Ostwald's and Ernst Mach's attacks on his ideas that he committed suicide. "And Georg Cantor, the originator of the modern theory of sets of points and of the orders of infinity, lost his mind because of the hatred and animosity against him and his ideas by his teacher Leopold Kronecker: he was confined to a mental hospital for many years at the end of his life."[7] The medical researcher Robert Gallo wrote vividly about the pain and shock of what he believed to be viciously harsh criticism.

> What surprised me were not the findings—as I say, I was already developing my own doubts—but the vehemence with which they were delivered. More than one speaker used our misfortune to ridicule the very idea of a human retrovirus. . . . Even now I have difficulty thinking back to that day. I would be subjected to far more extensive, personal, and even vicious attacks years later when I entered AIDS research. . . . But nothing compared

with the feelings that passed over me as I sat that day in Hershey, Pennsylvania, hearing not just HL-23 but much of my life's work— the search for tumor-causing RNA viruses in humans—systematically and disdainfully dismissed. . . . I was too old to cry, but it hurt too much to laugh.[8]

I am certainly not saying that we should all go out and be offensive or inflammatory just for the sake of it. Please don't paint swastikas on the synagogue and say I gave my blessing. I am against offending people for fun. But I am also only too well aware that in the pursuit of knowledge many people—probably most of us at one time or another—will be hurt, and that this is a reality which no amount of wishing or regulating can ever change. It is not good to offend people, but it is necessary. A no-offense society is a no-knowledge society.

If you want an example from life, take the case of Japan.[9] The Japanese have no tradition of open public criticism. In the traditional Japanese way of thinking, criticism was a mark of enmity; in fact, according to the intellectual historian Masao Maruyama, there was no word in Japanese for "opposition," as distinct from "enmity" or "antagonism," until one was imported from the West in the last century. That fact plus the society's emphasis on consensus and unanimity produced a climate in which people avoided criticizing each other. Pointing out someone's mistakes was considered rude, or worse. Change has been slow in coming. "An open debate is nearly impossible in this country," one Japanese economist told me when I visited Japan in 1990. A renowned political scientist said ruefully that the best policy toward ideas that you disagree with is one of benign neglect—to be mute. Criticism would be seen as an attack. Book reviewers typically don't review books they don't like. The result is that in Japan ideas tend to be traded on a kind of gray market. People criticize privately, exchanging gossip and asking each other "What did you think of so-and-so's new book on this or that?" Producing new ideas is hard, and testing ideas, sorting the useful from the empty, is harder. And so intellectual resources lie fallow.

The situation seems to be gradually improving. Yet there can be little doubt that the costs of the Japanese aversion to criticism have been enormous—not just for Japan but for the world. Japan is one of the world's largest, richest, best-educated, and hardest working nations. Yet she relies on outsiders to set her intellectual agenda; her universities are, by international standards, backwaters; her record on intellectual innovation is bleak. From 1901 to 1985 Japan won five Nobel Prizes in science—one twenty-eighth of America's share, one-tenth of Germany's. And has avoiding offense produced a better society? Not many American thinkers would want to live there, sitting expressionlessly through academic meetings. The price of the no-offense society is high.

Too many people today are forgetting this. They think you can keep knowledge and get rid of pain. They are epistemological pacifists, enjoying the products of critical inquiry while righteously condemning any unpleasantness which they see in the products' manufacture. A lot of them seem to think that intellectual goods grow on trees. A few years ago, a French course at Yale came under attack by a senior who brought it before the school's sexual harassment committee. Pierre Capretz, the designer of the course, had produced a kind of French-language TV soap opera ("French in Action"), which proved to be an immensely popular teaching aid; "dozens of public stations show it, and hundreds of universities use it as their basic French curriculum."[10] But the student was offended by what she regarded as sexual stereotyping—for instance, "a big picture of a woman from a French advertisement with half her shirt on." The student said, "It just really offended me to be in a classroom being portrayed in a completely objectified way." A lesbian student complained that "to have to sit through a sexist heterosexual romance every day as a way of learning French is very offensive." The students said that men might also be offended; the senior said that she "felt sorry for one balding student when hair vocabulary was the topic." It never seemed to have occurred to any of those people that the show was effective because it was fun, and that it was fun because its maker had ventured to be innovative and idiosyncratic, and that if he had been obliged to pander to everybody's feelings he would have produced numbing drivel. Then a lot of people who wanted to learn French would have been hurt.

A liberal society stands on the proposition that we should all take seriously the idea that we might be wrong. That means we must place no one, including ourselves, beyond the reach of criticism (no final say); it means that we must allow people to err, even where the error offends and upsets, as it often will. But we also are not supposed to claim we have knowledge except where belief is checked by no one in particular (no personal authority).

In other words, liberal science is built on two pillars. One is the right to offend in pursuit of truth. The other is the responsibility to check and be checked. Here, and here alone, is the social morality which finds error as fast as possible while keeping hurt to a minimum: intellectual license checked by intellectual discipline.

The discipline is just as important as the license—but it is important to remember what kind of discipline we mean. In February 1990 a part-time instructor at Indiana University–Purdue University at Indianapolis was fired after he told his Western Civilization class that "revisionists feel that this [the Holocaust] is complete nonsense." Some people do feel that way, of course. Some people also feel that the American landings on the moon were propaganda inventions staged by the U.S. government. But the lecturer presented the no-Holocaust view uncritically, as though it had checked out. The Nazis "did not gas anybody," photographs of stacks of bodies were doctored, "none of it makes sense unless you look at it from the prospect of Israel getting a lot of wealth from this story," and so forth.[11] It would be hard to think of anything more offensive to Jews, who were outraged. One Jewish leader called the lecture "not only a sacrilege to the memory of those who died, but to those who survived Hitler's death camps."[12] What to do in a case like this? The answer (I think) is that there is a right reason and a wrong reason to get this man out of the history classroom. The wrong reason is that his lecture offended Jews. No one has the right to be spared sacrilege—not Jews, not Muslims, not ethnic minorities, not me, and not you. The right reason is that he was teaching *as knowledge* a proposition which has been about as thoroughly debunked as any proposition could be. He should not be viewed as a man with an unpopular opinion (which he is, and which it is his right to be). Rather he ought to be viewed in the same light as a lecturer telling introductory biology classes that evolution is a humanist fiction, or telling introductory astronomy classes that Tauruses should play the lottery when Venus is in the house of Gemini. Now, I am the first to grant that in practice it is often difficult to tell the debunked from the offensive; we will have to argue. But the important thing is to keep our principles in sight: in a liberal society, to upset people is not, *and must never be,* the same thing as to be wrong.

And so when someone says he is offended, the standard reply should be: "I don't have to like you, but I won't shut you up or shout you down. However, I am not under the least obligation to take what you say seriously, or even to listen to you, unless you submit your claim to critical examination by me and others, and try to abide by the results."

What do you do about people who have silly or offensive opinions and who haven't bothered to submit to the rigors of public checking? Ignore them. Silence is science's most effective weapon. Any writer or scientist will tell you that he would rather be attacked than ignored. When someone says that the Holocaust didn't happen, why flatter him with attention? The world is always full of people who hold silly or obnoxious opinions and who have the means to broadcast them. That will never change. One of liberal science's great discoveries is that, provided such people are forbidden to use violence, the best strategy is to marginalize them unless and until they submit to proper checking. Ignored, they lose their megaphone.

And what should we require be done to assuage the feelings of people who have been offended, to recompense them for their hurt and punish their tormentors? This and only this: *absolutely nothing.* Nothing at all.

The standard answer to people who say they are offended should be: "Is there any casualty other than your feelings? Are you or others being threatened with violence or vandalism? No? Then it's a shame your feelings are hurt, but that's too bad. You'll live." If one is going to enjoy the benefits of living in a liberal society without being shamelessly hypocritical, one must try to be thick-skinned, since the way we make knowledge is by rubbing against one another. In a liberal culture, this is a matter of positive moral obligation. In practical terms, it means that people who get righteously offended twice every day before breakfast should learn to count to a hundred—granted, that takes discipline—and say to themselves, "Well, it's just that fellow's opinion," before they charge out the door crying for justice. (A sense of humor would help.) And it means that people receiving the complaints of the offended should count to a thousand before rushing out to do something about them. The alternative is to reward people for being upset. And as soon as people learn they can get something if they raise Cain about being offended, they go into the business of professional offendedness. Some people believe that the Russians are reading their minds with microwaves; other people fret about French classes that might inadvertently upset balding men. In a liberal society, the initial presumption ought to be that neither kind of concern deserves any better than to be politely ignored.

If that sounds callous, remember that the establishment of a right not to be offended would lead not to a more civil culture but to a lot of shouting matches over who was being offensive to whom, and who could claim to be more offended. All we will do that way is to shut ourselves up. The doctrine of Never Offend is the biggest reason so many Western intellectuals had so little to say when Khomeini went after Rushdie. The fundamentalists offended us, but one of our writers offended them first, so who's to blame? "We understand that the book itself has been found deeply offensive by people of the Muslim faith. It is a book that is offensive in many other ways as well. We can understand why it could be criticized," and so on.[13]

In one sense the rise of intellectual humanitarianism represents an advance of honesty: it drops the pretense that liberal science is a painless and purely mechanistic process, like doing crossword puzzles. But the conclusion which the humanitarians draw—that the hurting must be stopped—is all wrong. Impelling them toward their wrong conclusion is a dreadful error: the notion that hurtful words are a form of violence. Offensive speech hurts, say the humanitarians; it constitutes "words that wound" (writes one law professor); it does "real harm to real people" who deserve protection and redress (writes another law professor).[14] When a law student at Georgetown University published an article charging that the academic credentials of white and black students accepted at Georgetown were "dramatically unequal," a number of students demanded that the writer be punished. And note carefully the terms of the condemnation: "I think the article is assaultive. People were injured. I think that kind of speech is outrageous."[15] The notion of "assaultive speech" is no rarity today. Stanley Fish, a professor at Duke University, has said that "the speech that is being assaulted [on college campuses] is itself assaultive speech."[16]

A University of Michigan law professor said: "To me, racial epithets are not speech. They are bullets."[17] This, finally, is where the humanitarian line leads: to the erasure of the distinction, in principle and ultimately also in practice, between discussion and bloodshed. My own view is that words are words and bullets are bullets, and that it is important to keep this straight. For you do not have to be Kant to see what comes after "offensive words are bullets": if you hurt me with words, I reply with bullets, and the exchange is even. Rushdie hurt fundamentalist Muslims with words; his book was every bit as offensive to them as any epithet or slogan you can imagine. So they set out to hurt him back. Words are bullets; fair is fair.

If you are inclined to equate verbal offense with physical violence, think again about the logic of your position. If hurtful opinions are violence, then painful criticism is violence. In other words, on the humanitarian premise, *science itself is a form of violence*. What do you do about violence? You establish policing authorities—public or private—to stop it and to punish the perpetrators. You set up authorities empowered to weed out hurtful ideas and speech. In other words: an inquisition.

It is bad enough to have to remind people that there is no right not to be offended, and that criticism is not the same as violence. It is deeply embarrassing to have to deliver this reminder to people at the center of American intellectual life. The last few years have witnessed a rash of attempts on university campuses to restrict offensive speech, both by punishing offenders after the fact and by establishing preemptive restrictions. Most of the universities—certainly the private ones—were within their legal rights to set standards for behavior on their campuses. But universities are neither churches nor finishing schools: their mission and moral charter, their reason for being, is not to convert errant minds or to teach good manners. Their mission is to advance knowledge by teaching and practicing public criticism. Alas, many of them are doing exactly what a university, of all institutions, should not do: defining offensive speech as quasi-violent behavior, and treating it accordingly.

In 1989 the University of Wisconsin revised its student-conduct code to say that students would be disciplined for comments which "demean the [victim's] race, sex, religion, color, creed, disability, sexual orientation, national origin, ancestry or age," or which created "an intimidating, hostile or demeaning environment for education." One student got seven months' probation for telling an Asian-American student, "It's people like you—that's the reason this country is screwed up," "You don't belong here," and "Whites are always getting screwed by minorities and someday the whites will take over." Such statements, as federal judge Robert W. Warren noted in striking down the rule, express opinions. The University of Michigan adopted a six-page anti-bias code, likewise found unconstitutional, which provided for punishment of students who engaged in conduct that "stigmatizes or victimizes an individual on the basis of race, ethnicity, religion, sex, sexual orientation, creed, national origin, ancestry, age, marital status, handicap, or Vietnam-era veteran status."[18] It's hard to think what kind of social commentary might not be dragged in under one of those categories—especially given the university's enforcement guidelines, which gave as an example of discriminatory harassment, "A male student makes remarks in class like 'Women just aren't as good in this field as men,' thus creating a hostile learning atmosphere for female classmates." The guidelines said, "The University encourages open and vigorous intellectual discussion in the classroom. To reach this goal students must be free to participate in class discussion without *feeling* [my italics] harassed or intimidated by others' comments."[19] In overturning the university's rule, federal judge Avern Cohn noted that there had been three cases in which students were disciplined or threatened with discipline for comments made in a classroom setting.[20] The University of Pennsylvania forbade as harassment "any behavior, verbal or physical [note that speech has become "verbal behavior" here], that stigmatizes or victimizes individuals on the basis of race, ethnic or national origin . . . and that has the purpose or effect of interfering with an individual's academic or work performance; and/or creates an intimidating or offensive academic, living, or work environment."[21]

In other words, anyone who might make anyone else angry or upset, even inadvertently ("that has . . . the effect"), had better watch out. Tufts University wrote a policy which created three levels of allowable speech. "Varying degrees of expression are permissible on campus, depending upon the ability of others to avoid 'offensive' speech."[22] The University of Connecticut adopted rules punishing students for the use of "derogatory names, inappropriately directed laughter [!], inconsiderate jokes, and conspicuous exclusion [of another student] from conversation."[23] One official at Emory University was quoted as saying, "I don't believe freedom of speech on campus was designed to allow people to demean others on campus." Rutgers University adopted a policy against "insult, defamation, and harassment," written so as to encompass "belittling comments" and enforced against, for example, a student who publicly used the word "fag."[24] A student charging a Harvard Law School professor with sexism in a contracts course wrote, "A professor in any position at any school has no right or privilege to use the classroom in such a way as to offend, at the very least, 40 percent of the students."[25] (One wonders, would 10 percent be OK? How about 4 percent deeply offended, as against 40 percent mildly offended?) One can go on and on with the depressing litany. UCLA suspended a student editor when the paper ran a cartoon making fun of affirmative action; when a student editor at California State University, Northridge, ran an op-ed piece criticizing UCLA, he was suspended from the newspaper. At Stanford, a junior said, "We don't put as many restrictions on freedom of speech as we should."[26] On and on.

It is important to see that the Constitution is not, in those cases, the main issue. The Constitution can stop government institutions (like public universities) from punishing speech, but it does not proscribe attempts by private organizations to patrol their member-

ship for offensive beliefs. What proscribes that is the morality of
liberal science, with its commitment to public criticism of each by
any; but in the inner sanctum of our intellectual life, liberal morality
is fast being eroded by a misguided humanitarianism. I called some
professors I know to ask if there was really much to worry about.
They said that there was. A political science department chairman at
a leading public university said, "There are certain subjects which
can't be seriously discussed." The commitment on campus, he said,
is not to the free exchange of views, but "only to the free exchange
of acceptable views." Another political scientist told me, "We have a
freedom of speech problem on campus." At a prestigious private
college on the East Coast, a philosophy professor told me, "There's
an extreme chilling effect here among the faculty and the students
on the idea, right or wrong, that some of these minorities may be
responsible for some of their own problems." One side of a whole
variety of arguments is simply left out, he said.

    And how are restraints on offensive opinion justified? With argu-
ments that are appealing on the surface but alarming down below.
Trace their logic and you find that they all lead back to the same
conclusion: freewheeling criticism (thus liberal science) is dangerous
or hurtful and must be regulated by right-thinking people.
    "Why tolerate bigotry?" A classic argument, framed today in terms
like this: "Prohibiting racially and religiously bigoted speech is praise-
worthy because it seeks to elevate, not to degrade, because it draws
from human experience, not from woolly dogmas or academic slo-
gans, because it salutes reason as the backbone of freedom and toler-
ance."[27]
    That kind of rhetoric, besides being almost completely empty of
meaning, glides right around the important question: just who is
supposed to decide what speech is "bigoted" and what speech is
merely "critical"? What about the student at Michigan who was summoned to a disciplinary hearing for saying that homosexuality is a
disease treatable with therapy? Why is that a "bigoted" suggestion

rather than an unpopular opinion? What's the difference? And who is to say?

The anti-bigotry people never approach the question directly, because doing so would show them up. The answer is: *we,* the right-thinking, are the ones who will say who is and isn't bigoted.

Whenever anyone says that bigoted or offensive or victimizing or oppressing or vicious opinions should be suppressed, all he is really saying is, "Opinions which *I* hate should be suppressed." In other words, he is doing the same thing Plato did when he claimed that the philosopher (i.e., himself) should rule for the good of society: he is making a power grab. He wants to be the pope, the ayatollah, the philosopher-king.

The answer to the question "Why tolerate hateful or misguided opinions?" has been the same ever since Plato unveiled his ghastly utopia: because the alternative is worse.

"We don't want to block criticism and inquiry, just hate and intimidation." The trouble is the same: one person's hate speech is another person's sincerest criticism ("The Holocaust is an Israeli fabrication"). So who is to draw the line? Let's make up some examples. It is hard to see any redeeming social value in someone's saying "Niggers are stupid." But what about "On average, blacks are less intelligent than whites"? Should people who say that be punished? Then what about "Blacks display less aptitude for math, on average, than Asians"? If you clamp down on the first of those opinions, what do you do when someone complains about the next, and the next? Who will draw the fine distinctions?

It's no good, either, to proscribe epithets. Is "boy" an epithet, if a white man uses it to address a black man? When is it an epithet, when a term of affection, when just a mannerism? If an Anti-Epithet Board tried to decide such questions by looking at the particulars of each case—and each is different—it would soon be hopelessly entangled in ad hoc distinctions, conflicting testimony, and political mare's nests. ("In this case the addressee who was called 'boy' is a casual and usually friendly acquaintance of the addresser and is two years over the legal drinking age but looks much younger, and therefore a mitigating element of affection as well as an element of literalism may have been present. . . .") The alternative is to draw up lists of proscribed words; but that's no better. Put "nigger" on the list and you have proscribed *Huckleberry Finn*—unless you decorate your list with endless baroque distinctions, in which case you are hopelessly entangled again. ("Persons shall not use the word 'nigger' in direct conversation with black persons, unless the word is being used demonstratively or illustratively or both parties to the conversation are black or dark-skinned or the intentions are friendly as evinced by signs or gestures attesting to the conversation's mutual congeniality such as smiles, handshakes, or affectionate language. . . . Nothing in these rules shall be interpreted as proscribing *Huckleberry Finn* except when it is read aloud to a black person or persons in a taunting or confrontational manner, as evinced by undue emphasis on words such as 'nigger,' 'slave,' 'owner,' or when it is read in other circumstances which a reasonable person might regard as prejudicial and offensive. . . .") Meanwhile, of course, people who want to hurl insults will be busy inventing new ways to do so. They can always stay a step or two ahead of the list. The epithet guidelines would soon collapse.

Suppose, for argument's sake, that someone managed to discover a distinction separating hate talk from criticism as definitively as zero separates negative numbers from positive ones. Even that would be no guarantee of anything. The distinction might (or might not) satisfy philosophers, but in the political world ambitious activists would have every reason to smudge the line, stretch it, blur it, erase it, move it, or cross over it outright. And if they had support in the voting booths or in the student senate or in the streets, they would succeed. In politics the only distinction, finally, is between what you can get away with and what you can't.

Already—right from the start, in fact—humanitarians have tried to regulate theories and hypotheses as well as jeers and shouted epithets. After all, a theory can be just as hurtful as a jeer. At the University of Michigan, one administrator called for prohibitions on professors as well as students, saying, "Harassment in classrooms is based on theories held by teachers, and that environment has prevented minorities from having the same advantages afforded others."[28] In other words, hurtful theories should be suppressed.

The unhappy reality is that some people are always going to say gross and vicious things to hurt other people. If they don't destroy property or do violence, ignore them or criticize them. But do not set up an authority to punish them. Any guidelines elaborate enough to distinguish vicious opinions from unpopular ones will be too elaborate to work. In practice, the distinction will be between the opinions which the political authorities find congenial and those which they find inconvenient.

"In practice, we can distinguish verbal harassment from legitimate criticism by the hurtful intent of the speaker." No. In the first place, even the most "legitimate" criticism may be intended to hurt or discredit its target, as Robert Gallo, among many other scientists, knows well. In the second place, and more important: authorities that seek to punish the "intent" of criticism are even more dangerous than ones that seek to punish criticism itself. To establish the intent of words you must put the speaker's mind on trial. When the Michigan student said that homosexuality was a curable disease, did he intend to upset gay students, or not? That is the Inquisition indeed.

It is certainly true that the courts routinely weigh motive and intent in establishing, for instance, whether a killing was murder or self-defense, intentional or accidental. That is necessary and proper. But in the case of someone's telling a Jew that the Holocaust is an Israeli fabrication, the "crime" established by the intent is merely speech—criticism—and not violence. To make speech punishable on grounds of intent is to give authorities the power to punish criticism whenever they are suspicious of the critic. We should know better than to give any authority such power, least of all at a university. Certainly, then, there is no excuse for a university code like Stanford's, which prohibits speech that "is *intended* [my italics] to insult or stigmatize."

"Real people are being hurt, and so protective action is morally impera-tive." That people's *feelings* are hurt is undeniable. But one of the glaring failings of the never-offend movement—the same failing that

the anti-pornography movement always has to finesse—is its absolute inability to show any concrete, objective damage which offensive speech and opinions have actually done beyond damage to feelings. Nor have they been able to define how seriously one's feelings must be hurt to qualify one as verbally "wounded," or how to tell whether the victim of wounding words is really as badly hurt as he claims to be. How do you distinguish words that wound from words that annoy?

When pressed on this, humanitarians retreat to rhetoric about the way bigoted or vicious ideas are deeply repugnant, damage people's self-esteem, are a form of oppression, and the like. They argue that even to speak of hurtful words as "obnoxious" or "offensive" is to slight the words' damage. " 'Obnoxious' suggests that the injury or offense is a surface one that a large-minded ('liberated and humane') person should be able to tolerate if not embrace," writes Stanley Fish. "The idea that the effects of speech can penetrate to the core—either for good or for ill—is never entertained; everything is kept on the level of weightless verbal exchange; there is no sense of the lacerating harms that speech of certain kinds can inflict."[29] Note the retreat to the violence metaphor ("lacerating"). Note also the circularity: true, words "of certain kinds" can "penetrate to the core," but the whole question is which kinds and which words, and how do you tell, and how deep into the core is too deep? If we had an offendedness meter, then we might be able to solve that problem; as it is, the complaint that "real people are being hurt" does not begin to tell us who is being hurt, when, how badly, or how much is too much. Even if such a meter did exist, we would still have a problem: what about true words that "penetrate to the core"? What about useful but harsh criticisms that "penetrate to the core"? Suppose a creationist collapses in tears and drops out of college after a biology teacher declares that Darwin was right? Is that a "laceration"? Should it be stopped?

By and large, the humanitarians never even reach those questions, much less answer them. Beyond the rhetoric, all they are saying is this: "These ideas or words are very upsetting to me and to some others." Yes, they are upsetting. But if everyone has a right not to be upset, then all criticism, and therefore all scientific inquiry, is at best morally hazardous and at worst impossible. Even joking becomes impossible.

Faced with this problem, very often the humanitarians retreat to the position that *some* people—historically oppressed groups—have a special right not to be upset. That answer is no better. In the first place, it throws liberal science out the window, because it junks the empirical rule that anyone is allowed to criticize anyone, regardless of race or ethnic history or whatever. The fact that you're oppressed doesn't make you right. In the second place, who is going to decide who is allowed to upset whom? The only possible answer: a centralized political authority.

"It is hardly reasonable to justify here-and-now pain in the name of abstract principles or of knowledge which may or may not ever be produced." This is another humanitarian standby: hurting people in the name of abstract or future "freedom" or "knowledge" is like torturing people in the name of "God's word" or "your future salvation." "The requirement is that we endure whatever pain racist and hate speech inflicts for the sake of a future whose emergence we can only take on faith," writes Fish. "In a specifically religious vision like Milton's this makes perfect sense (it is indeed the whole of Christianity), but in the context of a politics that puts trust in the world and not in the Holy Spirit, it raises more questions than it answers and could be seen as the other prong of a strategy designed to de-legitimize the complaints of victimized groups."[30] In effect, abstract principles are all too often smoke screens for attacks on minorities.

Maybe they are; but we are not, in fact, talking about abstract principles or vague future gains. The trouble with the argument that real pain outweighs airy abstractions is that it leaves out one whole side of the equation: the pain is very real and very concrete for the "offensive" speaker who is sentenced by political authorities to prison, privation, or, as in Salman Rushdie's case, death. The whole point of liberal science is that it *substitutes* criticism for force and violence. That is to say, it substitutes the power of critics to select worthy ideas verbally for the power of political authorities to select "worthy" ideas forcibly. The false choice presented by humanitarians is between wounding people with words and not wounding people with words.

The real choice is between hurtful words and billy clubs, jail cells, or worse. If you think that the right to offend is a mere "abstraction," ask Rushdie.

"We're making the intellectual climate more free, not less free." The conventional wisdom now in many American universities seems to be that you can't have free thought or free speech where people, especially members of minority groups, feel intimidated, harassed, upset. Thus, if you get rid of talk which upsets or intimidates, you add to intellectual freedom.

Usually, that argument comes with high-sounding rhetoric of the following type. James T. Laney, the president of Emory University, was making the case for Emory's policy banning "discriminatory harassment," defined as "conduct (oral, written, graphic, or physical) directed against any person or group . . . that has the purpose or reasonably foreseeable effect of creating an offensive, demeaning, intimidating, or hostile environment." (Note, again, the implicit equivalence of speech and violence as two hurtful forms of conduct, "oral" and "physical.") Laney wrote: "Can the truth have its day in court when the courtroom is made into a mud-wrestling pit where vicious epithets are flung? And should the university be a place of such severe neutrality about values that mere volubility or numbers can carry the day?" He declared, "What we intend is not to curb free speech but to make it more probable."[31]

Leave aside, for now, the question of whether you actually can get rid of "intimidating" speech by slapping controls on it. Look instead at the premise of the argument: that you can only do science where people feel good about each other, where they feel secure and unharassed—in other words, where they are exempt from upsetting criticism. Of course, that is dead wrong. A lot of researchers and theorists hate each other. The history of science is full of bitter criticism and hard feelings; there is simply no way around it. If you insist on an unhostile or nonoffensive environment, then you belong in a monastery, not a university.

Look also at the Orwellian nature of the attack. It basically says that the more you stifle upsetting (e.g., "intimidating," "demeaning") speech and thought, the more "free" everybody becomes—so that the most "free" intellectual regime is the one with the most taboos on criticism.

The arguments of people like Laney sound good, because they appeal to our gut instinct that false and offensive opinions are a kind of immoral spewage which no good society should put up with. But it is important to remember where we have heard such arguments before: Plato. Society is lost if people with wrong opinions are allowed to go around spreading them. Such opinions "are ugly things" that lead citizens astray from truth, which is why people who hold them must be excluded from debate. As with Plato's policy, so with Emory's. The agenda is always the same: stifle ideas you hate in the name of a higher social good.

A footnote on a common rhetorical sleight-of-hand that fools too many people. Laney asks, "Should the university be a place of such severe neutrality about values that mere volubility or numbers can carry the day?" That is either a trick or an appalling misunderstanding. Liberal inquiry *is* a value, and *it*, not the promulgation of some particular group's notion of "truth," is the university's highest value.

"Without regulation, bad criticism will drive out good." That is, bigoted and vicious attacks will make reasoned debate impossible. Thus, regulation is needed to keep the critical discussion from blowing itself up.

Except in the very short run and among very small and confined groups, the truth is really just the other way around: good criticism drives out bad. If you want to be effective at the game of liberal science, you must persuade others that you are right; and, as a rule, abusive shouting is a poor way to make converts. For that reason, an epithet-shouting strategy is self-punishing except in the very short run. Why has science evolved such a mannerly demeanor? Not because scientists are better brought up than other people, but because thoughtful, systematic argument works better than "Nigger!" or "Faggot!"

What easily *can* blow up reasoned debate, of course, is the attempt to regulate it from the outside. If you think of cases in which critical argument really did break down—the Soviet Union, Nazi Germany, American McCarthyism, some American universities today on the

subject of race—you realize that the reason was that someone powerful acted to protect the society forcibly from "disruptive," "subversive,"
or "oppressive" words.

*"Equality in the marketplace of ideas must be attained before speech
can be truly free or debate can be fair."* The idea here is that, not only
is bigoted or vicious speech hurtful, it also silences its target, thus
violating the target's right to equal participation in debate. "Speakers
too can perpetrate repression aimed at victims whose voices in turn
are silenced, undermining equality and decreasing both individual
liberty and democratic dialogue," writes Mary Ellen Gale, a law professor. Just as markets need antitrust laws to prevent monopoly and
corruption, so debate needs equalizing measures, lest "dominant
groups devalue and subordinate the speech of others [and thus]
undercut any legitimate competition of ideas and stack the outcome
in favor of existing power and privilege."[32]

Even setting aside the constitutional issues—if Gale and others
are right, then the Constitution positively *requires* that the government
regulate speech—the problems here are endless. In the first place,
there is no right to "equal speech." We say what we like and are able
to say. Any other standard would require that the voluble be forcibly
silenced and the shy forced to stick their necks out. The feisty, the
keen, the aggressive and confident *will* talk more, but that doesn't
necessarily mean they will be the most effective. And to stop them
is to risk losing valuable criticism.

Second, the notion that criticism (as opposed to direct threats,
which no one thinks should be allowed either by governments or by
universities) silences its targets is flatly false. Some people, no doubt,
just roll over or slink away. But, of course, many more get angry and
argue back, far more strongly than if they had never been provoked.
Harsh, even vicious, criticism spurs just the sort of debate which
turns the heat of conflict into the light of knowledge. And so silencing
strong criticism does not "balance" an argument; it eviscerates it.

Third, and most important, there is, as always, the problem of
authority. Just who is supposed to say when speech is "equal"? Will
there be affirmative action for historically "silenced" minorities? Does
"equality" mean that blacks talk as much as whites, proportionately,
or more? That they be taken more seriously? How about creationists?

Do *they* get equal time? Who will decide? Obviously, an equal-speech regime inherently requires a strong regulative authority which can have no agreed-upon mission. So we are back, again, to the political regulation of inquiry on the behalf of the most politically powerful.

"The anti-harassment authorities will be neutral." In other words, if you establish a fair authority, criticism can be regulated fairly.

Sorry, but the hope is illusory and the record is abysmal. Does anyone seriously believe that today's university anti-discrimination committees would treat offended left-wingers and offended right-wingers the same way? Or that they would treat offended creationists and offended racial minorities the same way? The young editor at California State University at Northridge was suspended for running a cartoon critical of affirmative action; does anyone really think an editor would be suspended if he ran a cartoon critical of affirmative action's conservative opponents, even one depicting them as Neander-thals swinging from trees? Some people are offended by photos of white performers in blackface and others are offended by photos of gay sex; does anyone think that the anti-discrimination committees are equally likely to ban both from the university museum? And what about the day when right-wingers get the upper hand? Will *they* be "fair"? People who like authoritarianism always picture themselves running the show. But no one stays on top for long.

And what about people who are shocked and offended by charges that they are "bigoted" and "offensive"? They will come forward with their own claims. Any decision-making committee will inevitably have to favor one offended group over another. Neutrality is impossi-ble even in principle.

Recognizing that, some of the never-offend people have already said flat out that restraints on criticism and opinion should protect only "historical victim groups," whoever they are. (Should Jews be included? rich blacks? gay Republicans? tenured female professors making $60,000 a year?) So much for neutrality. Now we're in an argument over who should control inquiry. No one wins that kind of argument. Knowledge loses.

"The anti-harassment authorities will be wise." Maybe, maybe not. More likely, they will be politically powerful and determined to stay in power. In any case, wisdom is a shabby substitute for public

criticism. Most people would agree that Plato was among the wisest philosophers who ever lived, and look at what he wanted to do.

"Society will be better off with offensive and vicious opinions driven out." Many people say, "It's a shame we need to punish and drive out people who say and believe vicious things, but that is the price we pay to protect the civil from the uncivil and the oppressed from their would-be oppressors." In other words, you have to break a few eggs to make an omelet. The answer, as George Orwell said, is, yes, but where's the omelet?

The Inquisition failed to keep Copernicanism down. All it did was slow the progress of knowledge and kill people. The new inquisitions won't work any better. Attempts to suppress beliefs only succeed in calling attention to them and making them causes célèbres. The insistence that racist or homophobic or any other opinions not be tolerated only guarantees that any college sophomore can make the headlines by being outspokenly racist or homophobic, and for many sophomores the temptation is too much to resist. Nasty speech gets nastier as people get angry and start picking fights. Outrage escalates on every side. But nobody's mind is changed.

Every year hundreds of dense literary novels sell a few thousand copies and then sink into oblivion. Yet Ayatollah Khomeini managed to put one such novel on the best-seller lists. In America, thousands of scholars are working on thousands of research projects; most of them go unnoticed by everyone except specialists. Guess which scholar was the subject of a half-page, above-the-fold article in the *New York Times?* A researcher exploring "whether there are differences in intelligence between blacks and whites that help explain differences in their economic and social standing."[33] Liberal science declares that the issue of race and intelligence should be explored by any researcher who cares to explore it and who will follow the rules. But liberal science cannot guarantee a researcher half-page newspaper coverage. Only bans and taboos can do that.

"But we must take collective action to eliminate prejudice and bigotry." No, no, a thousand times no. We must take collective action to *check* prejudice and bigotry, that is all. What I said before is worth repeating: liberal science requires not that we be unprejudiced, but that we

have *different* prejudices. The authorities' role is not to get rid of prejudices but to protect criticism. The critical sorting system will do the rest. If central authorities care about advancing knowledge, as government and universities certainly should, then they may participate in public debate, but they must not try to regulate it.

It is, of course, admirable for *individuals* (as opposed to central authorities) to try to get rid of their prejudices. But there are two ways by which you absolutely cannot get rid of prejudice, even though both are very tempting. One, the method of Plato's philosopher, is to sit quietly in your room, thinking as carefully and objectively as you can and trying to clear your mind of prejudice. If you do that, you may feel that you are clearing your mind, but in fact you will be sinking deeper into your own stew. "Is it not a common experience," says Popper, "that those who are most convinced of having got rid of their prejudices are most prejudiced?" The second method, the political method of Plato's philosopher-king, is to find the most unprejudiced opinion in the land and instate it by force. Little more need be said about that method of eliminating prejudice.

The only reliable way to identify prejudice is through public critical exchange. If you want to think you're unprejudiced, you must *do* something: science. "What we call 'scientific objectivity,' " writes Popper, "is not a product of the individual scientist's impartiality, but a product of the social or public character of scientific method."[34]

"But doesn't the First Amendment protect us?" From government regulation of inquiry, yes. But not from ourselves, if we come to accept an ethic which obliterates the line between criticism and violence and so makes liberal science immoral in principle. If we accept the moral rightness of the humanitarian attack on intellectual liberalism, or of the egalitarian attack, then no First Amendment can save us.

"You're not black, or gay, or Hispanic, or whatever; you wouldn't understand." Only outsiders, only the oppressed, can understand the hurt, so only they can really comprehend the need for restrictions on debate. White males have no standing to protest controls, because they haven't felt the pain.

That argument deserves a special place in the hall of shame. For one thing, it assumes that only members of certified minority groups know what pain is like. Much worse, though: the only-minorities-can-understand argument is anti-intellectualism at its most rancid. It is the age-old tribalist notion that, as Popper put it, "we think with our blood," "with our national heritage," or "with our class." White supremacists will always say that blacks shouldn't be in charge because they "can't understand" (they're too stupid), anti-Semites will say the same about Jews (too corrupt), and now, shamefully, some American minority activists are saying something similar about "in-groups" (too pampered, too blind). They are denying the very possibility of liberal science, whose premise is that knowledge is available to everyone and comes through public inquiry and criticism, not from the color of your skin or your ethnic heritage or your social class. Accept their credo, and you have a race war or a class war where liberal inquiry once was.

Surely one of the nastiest little anti-intellectual tricks of our day is the use of the "thinking with one's skin" argument to justify affirmative-action policies. Now, affirmative action is something which reasonable people can well differ about, and in any case it is outside the compass of this book. However, proper justifications for affirmative action do *not* include the often-cited notion that affirmative-action policies will "include minority perspectives." One of liberal science's great social advances was to reject the idea that races or tribes have perspectives. Within any racial or ethnic group that you care to define, perspectives are much more different than alike. Knowing a man's color or descent tells you nothing whatever about his "perspective"; nor does it make him a bit more or less credible as a player in the game of science. No personal authority is allowed— nor any racial authority. To insist, then, on including people of various races as representatives of their "racial perspective" or "ethnic viewpoint" is to flirt with the irrationalism of Nazi science, and its distinctions between "Jewish" and "Aryan" science.

It is also to give power to ambitious and often dangerously illiberal people. Gays or blacks or women or whoever are no more in universal agreement than anyone else. When activists insist on introducing the "gay perspective" or the "black perspective" or the "women's perspective" into a curriculum or a discussion, they really mean introducing the activists' own particular opinions. Those minority activists want power and seek it by claiming to speak for a race or a gender or an ethnicity. Accept their premises, and knowledge comes in colors. Public criticism across lines of race or blood becomes difficult or impossible. Dinesh D'Souza records this amazing conversation—a snapshot of a possible future:

> I asked Erdman Palmore, [a sociologist] who teaches a course on race relations at Duke, what constitutes a black perspective. Palmore shook his head. "I have no idea," he said. "I am white. If I knew what a black perspective was, we wouldn't need blacks to provide it." Why then was he, a white man, teaching a course that engaged issues of black history and black consciousness? "It would be better to have a black teach my course," Palmore agreed. Did he think it was possible for a woman to teach Shakespeare? Palmore looked puzzled. "Oh, I see what you're getting at. He was a man. Yes, that is a problem. I don't know the answer, I must confess."[35]

"Well, it's not as bad as all that." Maybe not; maybe I'm too excited. But how bad is bad enough?

In a February 1991 survey by the American Bar Association, 60 percent of responding law students said that some professors do not tolerate different political beliefs; about 30 percent said that some professors are intolerant frequently or very frequently. Some students reported fearing reprisals if they were identified as conservative. In reporting the results, Steven C. Bahls, an associate dean at the University of Montana Law School, wrote that the reprisals "might be more imagined than real. Of course, whether these practices exist in reality is less important than what students perceive." Law schools, he wrote, "would do well to attack the problem of intolerance with the same vigor with which they attacked the lack of gender diversity and the lack of racial and cultural diversity."[36]

If anything, professors have better cause to fear their students than the other way around. At the University of Michigan, a respected demographer teaching his undergraduate course in "race and cultural contact" was accused of racial insensitivity. He chose to discontinue the course rather than stand in the line of fire.[37] Also at the University of Michigan, a student who read a limerick and made a joke about a famous athlete's being homosexual was required to attend gay-sensitivity sessions and publish a piece of self-criticism ("Learned My Lesson") in the student newspaper.[38] In 1989, at the University of Virginia Law School, one professor said to a black student in class, "Can you dig it, man?" The next day, visibly shaken, he read to the class from an anonymous note calling him a "racist" and a "white supremacist." He defended himself, but "eventually [his] eyes filled with tears. 'I can't go on,' he said," and rushed out of the classroom.[39] At the University of California at Berkeley, after a professor wrote in the alumni magazine that the affirmative-action program discriminated against white and Asian applicants, seventy-five students marched into his anthropology class and drowned out his lecture with chants of "bullshit"; one protester said that students "will not allow this kind of discourse."[40] At Harvard, a professor teaching a course on the history of race relations was accused of racism on such grounds as his use of a southern planter's diary and of the word "Indians"; rather than weather the attack, he stopped teaching the course.[41] At the University of Wisconsin, professors who issued a statement against what they called minority-hiring quotas were so frightened that only one of sixty-one would sign his name.[42] At the University of California at Santa Barbara, after filing a sexual-harassment complaint against a professor who referred in class to Penthouse "pets," a student said, "Maybe this will make more people aware in other classes and make other faculty watch what they say."[43] At Loyola University in Chicago, students demanded the dismissal of Professor Al Gini after he used the word "nigger" demonstratively in class. Several investigations ensued, in which Gini was questioned by four university offices and the U.S. Department of Education's civil-rights office. Though he was exonerated, he was quoted as saying, "I am deeply hurt, and if it were possible I think I would quit teaching." He no longer teaches affirmative action to undergraduates, and he says that "a lot of professors are taping their classes" in case they, too, are accused.[44]

Nat Hentoff relates how, at the University of Pennsylvania's Wharton School, a popular law lecturer named Murray Dolfman was explaining to his class why Americans can't be forced to work against their will. When no one knew that this doctrine comes from the

Thirteenth Amendment, he said, "We have ex-slaves here who should know about the Thirteenth Amendment." ("Neither slavery nor involuntary servitude . . . shall exist within the United States.")

The black students in his class did not know what was in that amendment, and Dolfman had them read it aloud. Later, they complained to university officials that they had been hurt and humiliated by having been referred to as ex-slaves. Moreover, they said, they had no reason to be grateful for a constitutional amendment which gave them rights which should never have been denied them—and gave them precious little else. They had not made these points in class, although Dolfman . . . encourages rebuttal.

Informed of the complaint, Dolfman told the black students he had intended no offense, and he apologized if they had been offended.

That would not do—either for the black students or for the administration. . . . Dolfman was banished from the campus for what came to be a year. But first he was forced to make a public apology to the entire university and then he was compelled to attend a "sensitivity and racial awareness" session. Sort of like a Vietnamese re-education camp.

A few conservative professors objected to the stigmatization of Murray Dolfman. I know of no student dissent. Indeed, those students most concerned with making the campus more "sensitive" to diversity exulted in Dolfman's humiliation. So did most liberals on the faculty.[45]

Though all of those examples come from universities, make no mistake: misguided humanitarianism is at work outside of universities as well. Think of St. Paul's stricken ordinance, which created the misdemeanor of placing "on public or private property a symbol, object, appellation, characterization, or graffiti . . . which one knows or has reasonable grounds to know arouses anger, alarm, or resentment in others on the basis of race, color, creed, or religion." Think of the many foreign laws and policies, mentioned in the first chapter, which regulate "hurtful" or "hateful" speech. Think of the journalists' lists of insensitive words ("Dutch treat—implies that Dutch people are cheap"). Think of the Hollywood producers who feel obliged to have their screenplays checked for "offensive" matter by minority activists. Taken together, the signs point clearly to the emergence of an anti-critical ethic.

Some of what has been going on recently can be understood as nothing more than a desire not to hurt people's feelings, or at least not to hurt the feelings of people viewed as especially vulnerable to social stigma. But that is not all that's going on. The picture goes from bad to worse when you throw the fundamentalist intellectual style into the mix.

A basic principle of science—of liberal social life—is that *we kill our hypotheses rather than each other.* Propositions are punished instead of their proponents. True, we often fail to live up to the principle despite our best efforts; that is inevitable. But the point is to try to distinguish the thought from the thinker. Karl Popper has pointed out that the critical method "consists in letting our hypotheses die in our stead." All species, he noticed, use trial and error, but humans do it in a special way. Animals look for mistaken "beliefs" (as it were) by living them through: wrong notions about where to find food, for example, tend to eliminate the organism along with the notion. Frogs that did not know what kind of bugs to eat would die off and be replaced by frogs that did know. Human knowledge can grow many, many times faster than animal "knowledge" because we can propose successive ideas and critically shoot them down without risking everything in the process. By trying out a billion propositions every day, and watching most of them fail, and then trying out another billion, a critical society becomes a huge error-seeking machine, able to find grains of gold in mountains of sand with astonishing speed. The machine works because, at least in principle, beliefs which fail to check out get the boot, but the people who propose them, if they acted honestly, do not. They are not (or are not supposed to be) banished or excommunicated or forced to sign a confession or required to submit to "rehabilitation." We all live, literally and figuratively, to try again.

Try explaining that to a fundamentalist. If the fundamentalist mindset has one ugly trait, it is the impulse to punish the believer along with the belief. After all, is not the believer denying the obvious, usually to the peril of the rest of us? Is it not obvious that a statement like "Blacks have watered down their genes because the less intelligent ones are the ones that have the most children" (the alleged Andy Rooney gem which I mentioned in the first chapter) is wrong? Is it not self-evident that such a falsehood—any falsehood, really—is dangerous? Could any decent, well-meaning person really believe such a thing?

Not long ago in America, punishing wrong believers along with wrong beliefs was the specialty of the right wing. That was what McCarthyism was all about. If you were a believer in communism, it was not just your belief, your "ism," which was bad, but *you*. You were a "Communist": not merely wrong in your political opinions but wrong, dangerous, and evil as a whole human being. You were not fit to live in American society. You were required to wear the scarlet letter C.

What the right wing did in those years was unforgivable. Now it is the left wing which has taken up where the right wing left off, a fact of which I could not be more ashamed. It is appropriate and entirely right to criticize propositions which we believe are false or immoral. But nowadays what you hear is less often a criticism of the proposition than of the person. We condemn not racism in particular but "racists"—whole human beings. A single offensive statement and you are marked as an evil believer, one whose beliefs can all be sealed together in a box stamped "wicked person"—one who has fallen from grace and who by rights should be turned out of society altogether. Apologize, reform, recant, or lose your job. In 1988 the law school faculty of the State University of New York at Buffalo warned students that if they made "ethnically derogatory statements, as well as other remarks based on prejudice or group stereotype," the faculty would take "strong and immediate steps" which would "not be limited solely to the use of ordinary university procedures"; the faculty resolved to write to "any bar to which such a student applies, including, where appropriate, its conclusion that the student should not be admitted to practice law."[46] That is what's known as blacklisting, and it is every bit as pernicious when law professors do it to people whom they judge to be racists as when McCarthyites did it to alleged Communists or when the Inquisition did it to alleged heretics. On university campuses, watch what you believe—one wrong opinion can get you branded a racist, a sexist, a homophobe, or all of the above. At the University of Northern Colorado in 1990, a former Reagan administration official named Linda Chavez was slated to give the commencement speech; her topic was the movement toward democracy in Eastern Europe and elsewhere. Then students and activists began to protest: Hispanic groups, the faculty senate, and the student government objected to her views on affirmative action and bilingual education—views wholly unrelated to anything she planned to talk about. She had the wrong kinds of beliefs and so was the wrong kind of person. The administration withdrew her invitation, and the president, Robert C. Dickeson, issued what Chavez justifiably called "an extraordinary statement": "The intent of the University in inviting Linda Chavez to be the commencement speaker was to be sensitive to cultural diversity and the committee making the decision intended to communicate the importance of cultural pluralism. It is clear that the decision was both uninformed and gave the appearance of being grossly insensitive." That kind of thinking seems to be becoming typical. The signs going up on doors across America say Evil Believers Not Welcome Here.

Andy Rooney strongly denied having made the comment about blacks' genes. But he had previously made a statement implying that homosexual intercourse was deadly. That was enough: to the righteous, he was one of the bad apples. David N. Dinkins, the mayor of New York, said that Rooney's denial was "tainted." "I find it difficult to believe that an individual who is apparently willing to embrace prejudice toward one group would not be capable of making prejudicial comments about another."[47] In other words, if you are evil enough to hold one wrong belief, nothing else you say counts.

That is execrable stuff. I hate to be Jeremiah, but let me say: In this kind of atmosphere, the way of inquiry will be blocked, knowledge will be the victim, and there will be no winners once the wheel has finished turning. The search for error will become a search for unorthodoxy.

In today's climate, it was no surprise when Mencken himself came under fire. The case was revealing of the mentality now at large. Mencken, who had a mean streak a mile wide, was accused of slighting blacks and (especially) Jews in his diaries, which he sealed until twenty-five years after his death and never intended for publication. In his heyday, Mencken was arguably the most powerful writer in America. He had every opportunity to use his public platform to defame blacks and Jews, but instead he did the opposite. The last article he wrote attacked a law that kept blacks off Baltimore's public tennis and golf courses: "it is high time that all such relics of Ku Kluxry be wiped out in Maryland." In the 1930s he denounced the United States and other countries for failing to open their doors to German Jews, saying that they should be brought to America and staked "sufficiently to set them on their feet." (How many lives might have been saved if more Americans had said the same thing?) Nonetheless, when the diaries were published, the attacks on Mencken came fast and hard. "Even a few drops of midnight poison are enough to damage Mencken's reputation seriously," wrote the *New York Times* book reviewer.[48] In the *Washington Post,* the writer Doris Grumbach denounced as an anti-Semite not only Mencken but anyone who might defend him: "those who defend a writer such as H. L. Mencken must be said to possess an antisemitic sensibility themselves."[49] The fact that the statements at issue had been made *in a diary,* the place where a writer keeps his most private thoughts, seemed to matter not at all. In other words, Mencken was condemned for *thinking* incorrectly—for turning out to have been an evil believer. Where ye find fundamentalist righteousness, there shall ye find the totalitarian idea.

One expects that sort of thing, of course, in politics and among people who in their working lives do not fashion themselves truth-seekers. But McCarthyism, in its day, never caught on among professionals in the knowledge business, among academics and journalists. Terrible it is to see that this time around the movement to condemn the mistaken along with their errors is widely respected among the

very people who most depend on the freedom to err. Intellectuals
are losing their nerve or their souls, or both.

The credo of liberal science imposes upon each of us two moral
obligations: to allow everybody to err and criticize, even obnoxiously,
and to submit everybody's beliefs—including our own—to public
checking before claiming that they deserve to be accepted as knowledge. Today, activists and moralists are assailing both halves of the
creed. They are assailing the right to err and criticize, when the error
seems outrageous or the criticism seems hurtful; they are assailing
the requirement for public checking, when the result is to reject
someone's belief. They have a right to pursue their attack (nonvio-
lently), but they, and we, should understand that they are enemies
of science itself, and even, ultimately, of freedom of thought. And
those of us who hold sacred the right to err and the duty to check
need to understand that our defense of liberal science must preach
not only toleration but discipline: the hard self-discipline which
requires us to live with offense.

6

Et Expecto Resurrectionem

As I write these words in 1992, more than three years have passed since the Ayatollah Khomeini's *fatwa* against Salman Rushdie. The British government has quietly resumed full diplomatic relations with Iran, although the death sentence over which the ties were severed has not been lifted. In August 1990 the British foreign secretary, anxious for Iran's cooperation in a multilateral effort to contain Iraq, made a point of praising Islam as one of the world's great religions and, in case anyone missed his point, added that Britain bore no responsibility for the publication of *The Satanic Verses*. Subsequently, the United States waged war on behalf of the government of Kuwait, one of the very few regimes that endorsed Khomeini's edict outright (Iraq condemned it). Since the affair began, the fundamentalists' rage had led to assassinations, riots, and bombings which had killed more than twenty people. "On a more mundane level," writes Daniel Pipes, "it led to a church being destroyed, book store windows being smashed, movies not distributed, and musical records withdrawn."[1] Bookstores were set on fire in Padua, Oslo, and Berkeley; a pipe bomb that was discovered in a Berkeley bookstore was found to have been capable of destroying the whole business and everyone in it. Moderate Muslims also were targets. Khomeini's message was not only for blasphemers in the West but also, no less important, for any among the faithful who might be tempted to apostasy. A letter from Karachi, Pakistan, to the *Observer* of London spoke for "those who are born Muslims but wish to recant in adulthood, yet are not permitted to on pain of death."

Someone who does not live in an Islamic society cannot imagine the sanctions, both self-imposed and external, that militate against expressing religious disbelief. "I don't believe in God" is an impossi-

ble public utterance even among family and friends. . . . So we
hold our tongues, those of us who doubt. . . .

Then, along comes Rushdie and speaks for us. Tells the world
that we exist—that we are not simply a mere fabrication of some
Jewish conspiracy. He ends our isolation. He ends it and simultaneously deepens it; frees us only to imprison us anew.[2]

In July 1991 the Italian translator of *The Satanic Verses* was stabbed
and wounded in Milan, and the Japanese translator—let history
record that the man's name was Hitoshi Igarashi, and that he was
only forty-four years old—was stabbed to death.

And Rushdie? Three years after the crisis began he was still living
underground. His marriage had broken up. Despite being shuttled
from one secret location to another, he had published another book,
and had popped up for brief appearances at a few bookstores. In
December 1990, apparently more out of desperation than conviction,
Rushdie announced to the world that he had embraced Islam.[3] "I am
able now to say that I am a Muslim," he wrote. All to no avail: from
Iran promptly came word that the death sentence was irrevocable.
The lesson of Rushdie's announcement, said Iran's spiritual leader,
the Ayatollah Ali Khamenei, was that "Western arrogance has been
forced to retreat step by step," and that "the edict, and the commitment
of Muslims around the world to implement it, is showing its first
results." The newspaper of the ruling Islamic Republican party said
that Rushdie's change of heart would better prepare him to meet his
maker. "He will die anyway, but he will be better off to choose his
way to eternal salvation courageously before a son of Islam fires the
coup de grace."[4]

In December 1991 Rushdie suddenly appeared at a dinner which
was being held at Columbia University to celebrate the First Amendment. (The British government was careful to keep its distance from
the trip, noting that although Rushdie had been given a berth on a
military airplane he would be expected to pay for his seat.) "It seems
to me that what's happened around me in the last thousand odd days
is a kind of parable about liberty," he said. "It's about the importance
of it and the danger of it. And so to be asked to speak at an event
which commemorates one of the great pieces of libertarian legislation

seemed like the correct place to say, to use an old line, that the price of liberty is eternal vigilance, that if you don't look out for and constantly redefend the rights you think you have, you lose them."

Rushdie said that he felt as if trapped in a bubble, "simultaneously exposed and sealed off." He spoke those words at a moment when the last of the Western hostages in Lebanon were being released by their captors. "I rejoice for them, and admire their courage, their resilience," he said. "And now I'm alone in the balloon."[5]

Biologically, at this writing, Rushdie is still alive. However, the death sentence has been carried out, for his life as a free man is over, and the day of resurrection is not yet come.

In my opinion, the Rushdie affair represented a turning point. It was a place from which it is possible to go in either of two directions and there is no standing still.

Khomeini's edict was bipartite. It was a sentence, namely death, for a crime, namely offending Muslims. Among the many possible reactions to the edict, two stand out. One, repudiate the sentence. Two, repudiate the crime.

If we repudiate the crime, then we say that Rushdie did nothing wrong. And if we say he did nothing wrong, then we must say, by implication, that others who offend—Americans who offend other Americans, for example—also do nothing wrong. Some people took such a position. But they did not include the major Western religious leaders. "No leading religious figure or organization stood by Rushdie in his hour of need," writes Pipes.[6] They also did not include the government of the United States. The president's statement went like this: "However offensive that book may be, inciting murder and offering rewards for its perpetration are deeply offensive to the norms of civilized behavior." The drift of the remark was not encouraging: the book was "offensive," the death threat was also "offensive," but one offense does not justify another.

The other course is to repudiate the sentence as barbaric and excessive, but not to repudiate the crime. People who offend should

perhaps be turned out or publicly shamed or fired from their jobs
or forcibly shut up. But death—death is too much, like chopping off
people's thumbs for shoplifting. This, I believe, is the path which a
great many Western intellectuals have chosen or are now tempted to
choose. If we follow this path, then we accept Khomeini's verdict,
and we are merely haggling with him over the sentence. If we follow
it, then we accept that in principle what is offensive should be suppressed, and we are fighting over what it is (pornography? homoerotic
photographs by Robert Mapplethorpe? disparagement of blacks? Darwinism? communism?) that is offensive.

No doubt equating criticism with violence is nothing new. Yet I
cannot help thinking we have been seeing more of it recently. For
instance, it has become routine to refer offhandedly to critics of Japan
as Japan-bashers. People do it now without a second thought—on
both sides of the Pacific. When I visited Japan, I would give speeches
pleading that criticism is not violence, that dropping bombs is violence, that if we suppress the former we will wind up with more of
the latter. Please, I said, let's stop talking about Japan-bashing and
America-bashing. Few of the Japanese, I discovered, had ever stopped
to consider that unpleasant criticism might be good rather than bad;
and I daresay few Americans have, either. In all cases, whether the
issue is race or Japan, the attempt to equate criticism with violence
is nothing more than an attempt to delegitimize and muzzle people
you disagree with. The result is predictable: the "Japan-bashers" strike
back by denouncing their opponents as "Japan-handlers," "agents of
influence" who work for Japan's interests rather than America's. So
now the whole debate has been poisoned, and nothing whatever has
been gained.

Stop; enough. The time has come for a reevaluation and a decision.
The time has come to look about us, collect our wits, and stand firm
on these principles:

No one is allowed the right to end any debate, or to claim special
control over it or exemption from it. No one under any circumstances
is exempt from criticism of any kind, however unpleasant.

No one will be punished for the beliefs he holds or the opinions
he states, because to believe incorrectly is never a crime.

Criticism, however unpleasant, is not violence. Except in cases where violence or vandalism is threatened or incited, the very notion of "words that wound" or "verbal harassment" is to be repudiated and junked.

Those who claim to be hurt by words must be led to expect nothing as compensation. Otherwise, once they learn they can get something by claiming to be hurt, they will go into the business of being offended.

We must all be sensitive not only to others' feelings but also to our obligations to liberal science: specifically, the obligation to put up with criticism—yes, offense—from any quarter at any time. We have a positive moral obligation to be thick-skinned. When we do become offended, as we all will, we must settle for responding with criticism or contempt, and stop short of demanding that the offender be punished or required to make restitution.

If you are unwilling to shoulder that obligation, if you insist on punishing people who say or believe "hurtful" things (as opposed to telling them why they are wrong, or just ignoring them), then you cannot fairly expect to share in the peace, freedom, and problem-solving success that liberal science is uniquely able to provide; indeed, you are putting those very benefits at risk.

Therefore, when offended people devote their energies to shutting someone up or turning him out or getting him fired, rather than trying to show that he is wrong or trying to be thicker skinned, we should be in the habit of telling them to grow up. That's all. No demands will be met, no punishments meted out.

Competitive and consensual public checking of each by each through criticism and questioning is the *only* legitimate way to decide who is right. Just as we need not apologize for the unique status of democracy and capitalism in our society, so we need not apologize for the hegemony of liberal science, even though many people will prefer other systems and demand at least equal standing for them.

No one who demands centrally enforced equal time or preferential treatment for his beliefs should be accommodated in the slightest, no matter how strong his political grievance. The fact that you're oppressed doesn't mean you know anything.

We must not tell creationists, Christian Scientists, and others that they are "loony"; we must not call them names. We must say, rather, "Your way of deciding what is true is illiberal and, if accepted, will substitute political turmoil or authoritarian control for peaceful and productive science."

Though we should all strive to eliminate or diminish our prejudices, the one and only way to do so is by submitting our beliefs to the rigors of public checking. Attempts to "eliminate prejudice" through political action or regulation of debate merely instate the favorite prejudice of someone powerful; all such attempts should be renounced, especially by governments and universities.

If we do not do our best to live by these principles, we will suffocate liberal science and block the way of inquiry, and so we will become the slaves of our errors, like Plato's pathetic philosopher-king.

At the beginning of this essay I mentioned two striking cases, one in France and the other in Michigan. As a codicil, there is something else I want to say about them.

I mentioned that the French passed laws banning Holocaust "revisionism," which questions and often denies that Hitler's genocide ever happened.

It so happens that I am a Jew. The idea of erasing the memory of 6 million dead horrifies me. The memory is all that stands in the way of Hitler's attaining his dream, which was not only to kill the Jews but to kill the very idea of them, to extinguish all traces, so that history would close up seamlessly around the gouge left by their extraction. It would be as though they had never existed.

Nonetheless—how hard this is to say—if some people want to erase the memory, they should go ahead and try. Stopping them from trying won't make anything any better. The only way is to let them have at it—while insisting that the only way they can succeed is through an exhaustive public process of checking, a process which

I believe will come as close as is humanly possible to sorting truth from falsehood.

How can a Jew say that? In the Museum of the Diaspora in Tel Aviv, written in large letters on the wall, I saw the answer: "A rabbi whose community does not disagree with him is not really a rabbi, and a rabbi who fears his community is not really a man." The quotation is from Rabbi Israel Salanter, who died six years before Hitler was born; he flourished in Lithuania and Russia, so almost certainly some of his descendants died in the Nazis' hell fires. I don't know what he would say about Holocaust "revisionism" if he were alive today, but I do know that those words of his are displayed in the Museum of the Diaspora because the critical spirit they embody is the only spirit that can save the Jews, and the rest of us, from political meddling with history.

At the beginning I also mentioned a case at the University of Michigan in which a student was disciplined for saying that he considered homosexuality a disease treatable with therapy.

Because of that wrongheaded idea, many gay people grow up hating themselves or living in fear. I know, because I am one of them. The no-offense humanitarians say of such opinions that they cause "real harm to real people." Yes. I have to agree.

Nonetheless, I am preaching that this student ought to be allowed to have his say, and that nothing at all should be done to stop him. If he wants to be rude about it, if he wants to post a sign on his door saying that "fags are sick," he should not be stopped. In fact, I am preaching that if he believes that gay people are curably ill, he should say so and try to prove his point.

How can I say that?

First, because punishing him won't work. No hypothesis has been laid to rest by suppressing it. The only way to kill a bad idea is by exposing it and supplanting it with better ones.

Second, because homosexuals, like all minorities, stand to lose far more than they win from measures regulating knowledge or debate. Today, true, the regulators may take gay people's side. But the wheel will turn, and the majority will reassert itself, and, when the inquisitorial machinery is turned against them, homosexuals will rue the day they helped set it up.

Third, because the liberal system is working. It has been bringing forth the truth about human sexuality from the murk of superstition and taboo. If homosexual political activists short-circuit the process by using intimidation and inquisition, the general public will soon see that universities are enforcing knowledge rather than searching for it. The researchers' credibility—science's credibility—will be shot. Prejudice then really will have the field to itself.

Fourth, because inquisitions are wrong, and because the advancement of human knowledge through the open-ended public search for error is much more important than my feelings. Though I have been told that I am "sick," though my feelings have suffered, I live a far fuller and happier life than I could in a society where powerful people's feelings were protected by an inquisition.

To the homosexuals—and blacks and feminists and Christians and so on—who want to silence the wrongheaded, I want to say: Yes, misinformation about homosexuality's being a "disease," or blacks' being inferior or whatever, does hurt people. But *all* misinformation hurts people. It used to be believed that human sacrifices helped the crops, that witches hexed villages and had to be destroyed, that bleeding the body was a good way to treat a fever. What hurts us is not wrong-thinking people but propaganda and ignorance; and unfettered criticism—liberal science—is the cure, not the disease.

I also said at the beginning: perhaps I'm too alarmed. If you now believe that I am overstating the dangers which fundamentalists, egalitarians, and above all humanitarians pose to liberal science, then so be it. But perhaps I have at least persuaded you to stay on your guard. That is important. As long as the game of science produces losers along with winners, as long as unfettered criticism makes people angry and hurt—so long will the enemies of liberal inquiry persist. In other words, forever. The danger will take new forms and clothe itself in new arguments, but it will not go away till the last trumpet sounds. Until then, let us remember Salman Rushdie and pray—no, fight—for his resurrection.

NOTES

Chapter One

1. Tony Katsigiannis, "How the NSW Anti-Discrimination Laws Threaten Free Speech," *Policy*, Summer 1989, p. 29.

2. *New York Times*, January 24, 1992.

3. Lindsy Van Gelder and Pamela Robin Brandt, *Are You Two . . . Together? A Gay and Lesbian Travel Guide to Europe* (Random House, 1991), p. 116.

4. Ronald Dworkin, "Liberty and Pornography," *New York Review of Books*, August 15, 1991, p. 13.

5. Barry R. Gross, "The Case of Philippe Rushton," *Academic Questions*, Fall 1990, pp. 35–46. In the end, the attorney general decided not to prosecute and settled for denouncing Rushton's ideas as "loony."

6. Quoted by Nat Hentoff in the *Washington Post*, op-ed page, July 21, 1990, and confirmed by the university's public-affairs office.

7. See, for example, Jon Wiener in the *Nation*, February 26, 1990, p. 272.

8. *New York Times*, May 6, 1990.

9. For historical information here and elsewhere I am indebted to Ronald L. Numbers's superb little essay, "The Creationists," in *But Is It Science? The Philosophical Question in the Creation/Evolution Controversy*, ed. Michael Ruse (Prometheus, 1988).

10. Duane T. Gish, "Creation, Evolution, and the Historical Evidence," reprinted from *American Biology Teacher*, March 1973, in *But Is It Science?* pp. 270, 281.

11. In *Edwards v. Aguillard* (1987). Chapter 5 has more on the case.

12. *New York Times*, November 10, 1989.

13. Beverly Slapin of Communities United against Racism in Education. Quoted in David L. Kirp, "Textbooks and Tribalism in California," *Public Interest*, Summer 1991, p. 27.

14. *A Curriculum of Inclusion*, Report of the [Education] Commissioner's Task Force on Minorities: Equity and Excellence, July 1989, opening words.

15. *New York Times*, February 7, 1990.

16. *A Curriculum of Inclusion*, p. 36.

17. Quoted in the *New York Times*, February 4, 1990.

18. "A Fringe History of the World," *U.S. News & World Report*, November 12, 1990, p. 25. Bracketed insertion is in the original.

19. "Science, Facts, and Feminism," in *Feminism & Science*, ed. Nancy Tuana (Indiana University Press, 1989), pp. 125, 126, 128.

20. *New York Times,* July 5, 1990.

21. Both trials ended in acquittals.

22. "Not a Moral Issue," in *Feminism Unmodified: Discourses on Life and Law* (Harvard University Press, 1987), p. 147.

23. As of this writing in 1992, the legislation has been approved by the Senate Judiciary Committee but stands well short of final passage.

24. Ronald Dworkin, "The Coming Battles over Free Speech," *New York Review of Books,* June 11, 1992, p. 61.

25. Wendy Melillo, "Can Pornography Lead to Violence?" *Washington Post, Health* section, July 21, 1992, p. 12.

26. *Feminism Unmodified,* p. 156.

27. Ibid., p. 148.

28. Ibid., pp. 154–55. Italics in original.

29. The quotations are from various essays in MacKinnon's *Feminism Unmodified,* pp. 130, 154, 147, 148, 154, 176.

30. "Hollywood's Sensitivity Training," *Washington Post,* December 28, 1991.

31. Quoted in the *New Republic,* February 18, 1991, p. 39. See also Walter Goodman, "Decreasing Our Word Power: The New Newspeak," *New York Times Book Review,* January 27, 1991, p. 14.

32. Quoted in the *Chronicle of Higher Education,* March 20, 1991, p. A-36.

33. *Newsweek,* February 12, 1990, p. 57.

34. His statement was quoted by Paul Berman in the *New Republic,* October 8, 1990. The rabbi, Immanuel Jakobovits, was writing in the *Times* (London), March 4, 1989.

35. Quoted by Robert R. Detlefsen in the *New Republic,* April 10, 1989, p. 19.

36. *Newsweek,* February 12, 1990, p. 53.

37. February 13, 1990, p. C-18.

38. *Washington Post,* January 20, 1991.

39. December 31, 1990, and January 20, 1991.

40. *Chicago Sun-Times,* March 23, 1991.

41. *The Economist,* October 5, 1991, p. 36. Iqbal's lawyer said that his client had done nothing except underline passages in the Koran.

42. Judith Martin and Gunther Stent, op-ed page, March 20, 1991.

43. Khomeini interview with Oriana Fallaci, *New York Times Magazine,* October 7, 1979, p. 31.

Chapter Two

1. All references in parentheses are to *The Republic,* trans. Paul Shorey, in *Collected Dialogues,* ed. Edith Hamilton and Huntington Cairns (Princeton University Press, 1961).

2. *Theaetetus,* 173e and 174c, trans. F. M. Cornford, in *Collected Dialogues.*

3. From Raymond A. Moody, Jr., *Elvis after Life: Unusual Psychic Experiences Surrounding the Death of a Superstar* (Atlanta: Peachtree, 1988). Excerpted in *Harper's*, August 1988.

4. *Wall Street Journal*, September 8, 1988.

5. *Theaetetus*, 169b, 158d.

6. Ibid., 179b.

7. Second *Meditation on First Philosophy*, trans. Norman Kemp Smith (Random House, 1958).

8. On the skeptical crisis of the sixteenth and seventeenth centuries, see Richard H. Popkin, *The History of Scepticism from Erasmus to Descartes* (Humanities Press, 1964).

9. *Apology for Raymond Sebond*, in *Complete Essays*, trans. Donald M. Frame (Stanford University Press, 1958), pp. 423, 424, 447, 421.

10. *A Treatise of Human Nature*, book I, part iv, section 12, and I:ii:6, in the Oxford edition (1978), pp. 139, 67.

11. "The Sentiment of Rationality" (1879).

12. *Infinite in All Directions* (Harper & Row, 1988), p. 11. The motto is taken from a line of Horace, *Nullius addictus iurare in verba magistri*, or "I am not bound to revere the word of any particular master"—a splendid statement of the scientific ethic.

13. "The Two Faces of Common Sense," in *Objective Knowledge: An Evolutionary Approach* (Oxford, 1972), p. 77.

14. *A Brief History of Time* (Bantam Books, 1988), p. 94.

15. Quoted by Philip P. Wiener in his preface to Peirce's *Selected Writings*, ed. Wiener (Dover, 1966).

16. From Peirce's letter to Lady Welby of December 23, 1908, ibid., p. 398.

17. Sandra Harding, *The Science Question in Feminism* (Cornell University Press, 1986), p. 25.

Chapter Three

1. *The Panda's Thumb: More Reflections in Natural History* (W. W. Norton, 1980), p. 67.

2. *Second Treatise of Government*, section 223 and following.

3. *Essay Concerning Human Understanding* (1690), book 4, chap. 20, section 17; chap. 19, section 12.

4. Ibid., chap. 16, section 4.

5. The greatest statement of this point is J. S. Mill's: "However unwillingly a person who has a strong opinion may admit the possibility that his opinion may be false, he ought to be moved by the consideration that however true it may be, if it is not fully, frequently, and fearlessly discussed, it will be held as a dead dogma, not a living truth" (*On Liberty*, chap. 2).

6. *Essay*, book 4, chap. 19, section 11.

7. *Science and Philosophy: Past and Present* (Penguin, 1989), pp. 41, 42.

8. *Apology for Raymond Sebond,* in *Complete Essays,* trans. Donald M. Frame (Stanford University Press, 1958), pp. 421, 428.

9. *A Turn in the South* (Alfred A. Knopf, 1989), p. 295.

10. March 30, 1988.

11. *Objective Knowledge: An Evolutionary Approach* (Oxford University Press, 1972), p. 70.

12. June 13, 1989.

13. *Science as a Process* (University of Chicago Press, 1988), p. 22.

14. *Wall Street Journal,* August 28, 1989.

15. *Science as a Process,* p. 163.

16. August 15, 1989.

17. *Principles of Geology,* 4th ed. (London), p. 87.

18. From an unsigned review, attributed to John Playfair, in the *Edinburgh Review* 19 (November 1811): 207.

19. *A Geological Essay on the Imperfect Evidence in Support of a Theory of the Earth* (1815), p. 269.

20. Attributed to Playfair, *Edinburgh Review* 19, p. 208.

21. Review, attributed to William Fitton, in the *Edinburgh Review* 29 (October 1923): 198.

22. *Little Science, Big Science . . . and Beyond* (Columbia University Press, 1986), pp. 1, 8. The book was first published in 1963, the "now" of which Price writes.

23. Organization for Economic Cooperation and Development, *Science and Technology Policy Outlook, 1988,* p. 33.

24. *Pluto's Republic* (Oxford, 1982), p. 80.

25. April 24.

26. "The Perils of Absolutism," Speech at Brown University, *Brown Alumni Monthly,* May 1989, p. 38.

27. *Science, Faith and Society* (University of Chicago Press, 1946), p. 16.

28. *New York Times,* July 14, 1989.

29. In *Selected Writings,* ed. Philip P. Wiener (Dover, 1966), p. 103.

30. *After Virtue: A Study in Moral Theory,* 2d ed. (University of Notre Dame Press, 1984), pp. 236, 250–51.

31. Ibid., p. 252.

32. Ibid., p. 263.

Chapter Four

1. *New York Times Magazine,* October 7, 1979, p. 31.

2. *Essay Concerning Human Understanding,* book 4, chap. 19, sections 8, 6.

3. *On Certainty,* trans. Denis Paul and G. E. M. Anscombe, ed. Anscombe and G. H. von Wright (Harper & Row, 1972), nos. 96, 95, 497.

4. Bradley R. Smith, *Confessions of a Holocaust Revisionist,* as quoted in the *New York Times,* December 23, 1991.

5. Avishai Margalit, "Israel: The Rise of the Ultra-Orthodox," *New York Review of Books,* November 9, 1989, p. 43.

6. July 9, 1989.

7. *American Lawyer,* June 1989.

8. He was quoted by Mark Shields in the *Washington Post,* op-ed page, November 29, 1987.

9. *New York Times,* November 25, 1988.

10. Quoted by Bruce B. Lawrence, *Defenders of God: The Fundamentalist Revolt against the Modern Age* (Harper & Row, 1989), p. 183. Lawrence, in turn, cites Northrup Frye's *The Great Code: The Bible and Literature* (Harcourt Brace Jovanovich, 1982), p. 10.

11. *Wall Street Journal,* September 13, 1988.

12. *New York Times Magazine,* p. 31.

13. Ibid.

14. *The Republic,* trans. Paul Shorey, in *Collected Dialogues,* ed. Edith Hamilton and Huntington Cairns (Princeton University Press, 1961), 399a.

15. *Washington Post,* October 6, 1989.

16. *New York Times,* July 5, 1989.

17. Quoted in the *Los Angeles Times,* January 26, 1989.

18. *New York Times,* June 15, 1982.

19. *Washington Post,* October 14, 1989.

20. "Evangels of Abortion," in the *New York Review of Books,* June 15, 1989.

21. Romans 1:18–20.

22. *The Crisis of Parliaments: English History 1509–1660* (Oxford University Press, 1971), p. 141.

23. The Chinese astrophysicist and dissident Fang Lizhi in the *New York Review of Books,* February 2, 1989, p. 3.

24. See Amalrik, *Notes of a Revolutionary* (Weidenfeld and Nicolson, 1982).

Chapter Five

1. *New York Times,* June 20, 1987.

2. *A Curriculum of Inclusion,* Report of the [Education] Commissioner's Task Force on Minorities: Equity and Excellence, July 1989, p. 34.

3. Quoted in the *New York Times,* February 4, 1990.

4. Teaching belief *as belief* is something else again. I have no objection to teaching: "We now know that Homo sapiens evolved from other species. Some people, however, don't believe it. We also know that Elvis is dead. Some people don't believe it." Seculars' attempts to keep all teaching about religion out of the public schools have been misguided. Religion is important in American life and should be taught—as belief rather than as knowledge.

5. A. S. Turberville, *The Spanish Inquisition* (Thornton Butterworth, 1932), p. 3.

6. *Science as a Process* (University of Chicago Press, 1988), p. 30.

7. S. Chandrasekhar, *Truth and Beauty: Aesthetics and Motivations in Science* (University of Chicago Press, 1987), p. 24.

8. In Gallo's *Virus Hunting—AIDS, Cancer, and the Human Retrovirus: A Story of Scientific Discovery* (Basic Books, 1991), pp. 85–86.

9. For more on the Japanese intellectual system, see the author's *The Outnation: A Search for the Soul of Japan* (Harvard Business School Press, 1992), which I draw on here.

10. *Washington Post,* February 11, 1990.

11. *Indianapolis Star,* February 16, 1990.

12. Ibid., February 20, 1990.

13. This was Sir Geoffrey Howe, the British foreign secretary, two weeks after Khomeini decreed Rushdie's death sentence. Earlier, Howe's American counterpart, James A. Baker III, reacted to the threat by going so far as to call it "regrettable." To Britain's credit, however, it did stand by Rushdie in protecting his physical safety.

14. The quotations are from (respectively) Richard Delgado of the University of Wisconsin Law School and Mari Matsuda of Stanford Law School, both quoted in Jon Wiener, "Free Speech for Campus Bigots?" *The Nation,* February 26, 1990, p. 273.

15. *Washington Post,* April 17, 1991. The quotation is from a second-year student named Gillian Caldwell.

16. From an interview on "The MacNeil/Lehrer Newshour," June 19, 1991.

17. Quoted in Dinesh D'Souza, *Illiberal Education: The Politics of Race and Sex on Campus* (Free Press, 1991), p. 152.

18. For the Michigan and Wisconsin cases, see Chester E. Finn, Jr., in *Commentary,* September 1989. He goes on to list other such rules.

19. On the Michigan situation, see D'Souza.

20. Wiener, p. 274.

21. Quoted by Alan Charles Kors writing in the *Wall Street Journal,* October 12, 1989.

22. Melissa Russo (a Tufts senior who opposed the rule), writing in the *New York Times,* September 27, 1989.

23. Wiener, p. 273.

24. Policy quoted courtesy of the Rutgers University news office. On the "fag" incident, see the *Wall Street Journal,* February 3, 1992.

25. Emory and Harvard cases in Finn.

26. Quoted in the *New York Times,* December 11, 1989.

27. This is the conservative legal scholar Bruce Fein, writing in the *Washington Times,* May 1, 1990.

28. D'Souza, p. 141.

29. "There's No Such Thing as Free Speech and It's a Good Thing Too," *Boston Review,* February 1992, p. 24.

30. Ibid.

31. Writing in the *New York Times,* op-ed page, April 6, 1990.

32. "On Curbing Racial Speech," in *The Responsive Community* 1, no. 1 (Winter 1990–91): 51, 54, 55.

33. November 30, 1990.

34. Both quotations are from *The Open Society and Its Enemies* (Princeton University Press, 1966), vol. 2, pp. 223 and 220, respectively.

35. D'Souza, p. 186.

36. Ken Meyers, "Survey: Students Loath to Differ Politically with Their Professors," *National Law Journal,* February 10, 1991, p. 4.

37. Finn, p. 19.

38. John Taylor, "Are You Politically Correct?" *New York Magazine,* January 21, 1991, p. 35.

39. D'Souza, pp. 5–6.

40. "Taking Offense," *Newsweek,* December 24, 1990, p. 50; and *Washington Post,* May 27, 1991.

41. Taylor, pp. 33–34.

42. *Newsweek,* December 24, 1990, p. 52.

43. Taylor, p. 37.

44. *Chicago Sun-Times,* March 11, 1991.

45. "Free Speech on Campus," *The Progressive,* May 1989, p. 13.

46. See Nat Hentoff in *Reason,* November 1991, p. 33; and D'Souza, p. 9.

47. Quoted in the *New York Times,* February 13, 1990.

48. Herbert Mitgang, January 1, 1990.

49. July 12, 1990.

Chapter Six

1. Daniel Pipes, *The Rushdie Affair: The Novel, the Ayatollah, and the West* (Birch Lane, 1990), p. 16.

2. March 12, 1989. Quoted in ibid., p. 151.

3. "Rushdie later called [this declaration] a mistake, said he'd been double-crossed in a bargain to which he'd been led by desperation." Amy E. Schwartz writing in the *Washington Post,* op-ed page, April 2, 1992.

4. *New York Times,* December 27 and 28, 1990.

5. *New York Times,* December 12, 1991.

6. Pipes, p. 165.

INDEX

Affirmative action, 146
Amalrik, Andrei, 109
Anti-Discrimination Act, Australia, 1–2
Anti-harassment rules, 3
Authoritarianism
  as alternative to liberal science, 28–29
  intellectual, 26, 97, 99
  of Plato's *Republic*, 31–35, 41
Authoritarians
  effect of science rules on, 76, 78
  intellectual regimes of, 64–65
  as political enemies, 4
  weak system of, 74

Bahls, Steven C., 147
Baker, Howard, 35
Beliefs
  diversity of, 64
  fixed, 94–99, 102
  freedom of, 116–17
  insistence on freedom of, 131–32
  in liberal science, 101–2
  punishment for, 151–53
  respectability of, 120
  sorting true from false, 5–6
  submission to public checking, 154
  that cause pain, 121–22
  uncheckable, 81–82
  unrestricted by liberal science, 116
Bias, 67–68
Bill of Rights, 60
Boltzmann, Ludwig, 125
Bryan, William Jennings, 7, 98
Bush, George, 20

Cantor, Georg, 125
Capitalism, 27, 63, 86, 90
  See also Markets
Capretz, Pierre, 127

Certainty
  fundamentalists' search for, 94–96
  in Hume's philosophy, 44–45
  in liberal science, 45
Chavez, Linda, 152
Checking
  of beliefs, 116–17
  in liberal science, 66, 68–70, 73–75, 128
  process of, 119
  See also Public checking
Cohn, Avern, 132
Compassion, 14
Conflict
  generating and resolving, 64–65, 73–74
  handled by liberalism, 57
  settlement according to Plato, 40, 42
Consensus
  can reject beliefs, 117
  deciding what is, 117–19
  Japanese emphasis on, 126
  in liberal science, 101–2
  in scientific conclusions, 58
Creationist theory, 7–12, 21, 29, 38, 114, 115
Creed wars
  beginnings of, 119
  in critical society, 77
  disputes leading to, 72
Criticism
  across racial or blood lines, 146–47
  advancement by Descartes of, 44
  effect of silencing, 142
  enduring, 125–28
  good, 141
  is not violence, 131, 158–59
  Japanese avoidance of, 126

morality of, 106–10
Plato's version of, 31
See also Plato

Gale, Mary Ellen, 142
Gallo, Robert, 125–26, 137
Game-playing (for decision-making),
    50
Gjertsen, Derek, 62
Global warming, 119
Goldwater, Barry, 106
Goodman, Walter, 23
Gould, Stephen Jay, 58–59, 68–69
Grumbach, Doris, 153

Hate-crime laws, 24–25
Hawking, Stephen W., 51–52
Hentoff, Nat, 148
Homosexuals, 161–62
Hubbard, Ruth, 12
Hull, David L., 67, 69–70, 124
Humanitarianism
    attack on liberal science, 121
    misguided, 149–50
    new intellectual, 124–25
    at university level, 146–49
Humanitarian Principle, 6
    challenge to liberal science from,
        27
    in Khomeini decree, 21
    view of speech as form of violence,
        25–26
Humanitarians
    false choice presented by, 139
    goal of, 28
    opposition to liberal intellectual
        system, 19–22
    as political enemies, 4
    regulation by, 136–37
    suppression tendencies of, 123–24
Hume, David
    arguments against Plato's ideas, 31
    on induction, 44
Hymers, Robert L., 94

Igarashi, Hitoshi, 156

Imperialism (of liberal, scientific view),
    12–14
Infallibility, papal, 56
Inquisition
    circumstances leading to, 27
    in circumstances of offensive
        speech, 3–4
Inquisition, the
    argument of, 123
    conditions for end of, 78
    effect of, 144
    revival of idea of, 6
Interchangeability (of persons), 53
Intolerance, 147–49

James, William, 46
Jesus, 79
John Paul II (pope), 78

Kant, Immanuel, 53
Khamenei, Ayatollah Ali, 156
Khomeini, Ayatollah Ruhollah
    decree against Rushdie, 20–21,
        111, 155
    on his access to truth, 89
    on Islam, 99
    on prohibition of some kinds of
        music, 100
    on technology, 29–30
Kidd, John, 71
Knowledge
    creation of, 125–27, 129
    established claim of, 118–19
    evolutionary view of, 58
    hunt for error in, 51–52
    is a product, 39
    liberal, scientific view of, 12–13
    prescription to advance, 19
    production of in Plato's *Republic*,
        33–34
    public, 80–81
    questions surrounding, 35–36
    rejection of freedom of, 13–14
    restricted by liberal science,
        116–17
    source of, 33–34
    tentative nature of, 45–46

ABOUT THE AUTHOR

Jonathan Rauch is a contributing editor of the *National Journal* and the author of *The Outnation: A Search for the Soul of Japan.* His writings have appeared in many publications, including the *Atlantic,* the *New Republic,* the *Los Angeles Times,* and the *New York Times.*